Protecting and Maintaining Retirement Income Throughout The Looming Financial Crisis

By Jeffrey D. Voudrie, CFP®
Copyright 2013

Disclaimer:

All statistics and references to specific products mentioned in this book are based on materials believed to be reliable, and are subject to change. This book may speak in generalities; specific riders and features of annuities will differ from company to company. Always read the prospectus before investing in any annuity.

All information contained in this book is for informational purposes only and does not constitute a solicitation or offer to buy or sell securities or investment advisory services. While every effort has been made to offer the most current and correct information possible, inadvertent errors can occur, and the specific facts of each individual's situation may change the results and recommendations provided in this book. It should also be noted that certain statements and assertions of fact in this book may also be impacted by local, state or federal laws, rules and regulations. The accuracy, completeness or timeliness of the information contained in this book cannot be guaranteed.

The information provided is not intended to serve as legal, accounting or tax advice; you are strongly encouraged to consult with qualified attorneys, accountants and other financial professionals for advice concerning specific matters before making any decision. Jeff Voudrie, nor Common Sense Advisors, does not represent, warrant or guarantee, or assume any liability in respect of results based on the use of the information in this book.

TABLE OF CONTENTS

Disclaimer.. 2

About the Author.. 5

Other Books by Jeff Voudrie................................. 7

Introduction.. 13

Chapter One:
The Help You Need in Today's Economic Climate 15

Chapter Two:
What You Need to Change 24

Chapter Three:
Pre-packaged Investment Products Are NOT What They Seem ... 43

Chapter Four:
How and Why Traditional Investments Are
the Right Choice in a Non-Traditional Era................... 48

Chapter Five:
Do You Need the Help of a Financial Pro?
Choosing Between Good, Better and Best 53

Chapter Six:
The Pros and Cons of Working with a
New-Era Private Money Manager 68

Chapter Seven:
Retain Full Control of Your Money AND
Get the Guidance You Need 82

A Word on Faith 91

About the Author

Jeff Voudrie (pronounced "Voo-DRAY") is a Certified Financial Planning Professional® and a nationally recognized financial advisor whom many consider an expert in how annuities work. He is known for his straightforward, easy-to-understand (and often opinionated) writing style. He's been interviewed by many prestigious publications, including *The Wall Street Journal, CBS Marketwatch, Kiplinger, The London Financial Times, The Christian Science Monitor, CFO.com* and *Financial Planning Magazine*. Jeff has also appeared on CNNfn as an expert and wrote the nationally syndicated weekly financial column, *Guarding Your Wealth*.

Jeff began his career in the financial services industry dating back to the crash of 1987 and started his own firm in 2001. The Bear Market of 2001-2002 caused him to develop unique trading systems and software to utilize dynamically responsive portfolio management and real-time portfolio monitoring that earned him the issue of three U.S. Patents.

On a personal note, Jeff and his wife of 27 years, Julie, are the proud parents of seven children—three of them adopted from Ethiopia in 2009. Having served as overseas missionaries, being very involved in their local church (you can learn more about Jeff's faith at the end of this book) and homeschooling their children, Jeff and Julie's personal faith is reflected in everything they do. That includes Jeff's approach to his business, where he takes seriously his responsibility to protect, empower and educate investors. Julie and his oldest daughter Danielle appeared on TLC Network's "Next Great Baker" Season 4, which aired internationally in June 2014.

You can learn more about Jeff at http://JeffVoudrie.com or contact him at Jeff@CommonSenseAdvisors.com.

**Other Books by Jeff Voudrie from
The Retired Investor's Survival Guide Series:**

Why Variable Annuities Don't Work the Way You Think:

Hidden Dangers That Can Devastate Retirees ($9.99)

Annuity salespeople certainly know how to deliver a persuasive sales pitch. This report is designed to give you the other side of the variable annuity story. My viewpoint is unique and, quite frankly, goes against the industry grain. Granted, many respected advisors firmly believe that variable annuities are good for consumers;my opinion is quite different. In the end, only you can decide what is best for your situation. However, if you don't know all the facts, how can you make an informed decision?

In this book I give you facts you can't readily find anywhere else, certainly not from the advisors that sell variable annuities. Once you've read this book, you will no longer be an easy mark for commission-hungry advisors, and you will discover better ways to invest that will put you in control of your financial future and get you ahead of the game in the long haul.

Let me tell you right up-front that this book is biased--I am not trying to present a balanced discussion of the advantages and disadvantages of variable annuities. My purpose in this book is to provide a contra-argument to the presentations for these products that you've likely already heard from the financial services industry.

I'll be frank: I'm not going to pull my punches. IF you choose to buy a variable annuity, you should do so knowing all of the facts and, more importantly, the implications of those facts. I do not like variable annuities and have not recommended them to a client for years.

In this book, I will go into great detail explaining:

1. What is a Variable Annuity?
2. How You Think They Work, How They Really Work
3. Hidden Costs, Hidden Dangers
4. Alternatives and Better Choices

One of the most highly touted benefits of variable annuities these days is the Living Benefit Rider, which guarantees a lifetime income stream. These are often accompanied by a provision that most investors believe guarantees they will earn at least 6% or 7%. If you have been pitched a variable annuity and are particularly attracted to it because of this benefit, then you can skip straight to my discussion of it on page 8. You'll quickly learn that the way you think it works may be considerably different from the way it actually does.

From start to finish, you should be able to digest this book in an hour or less.

How Successful Investors Tripled The Return of the S&P 500:

The SECRET to Stop Playing By Wall Street's Rules, End Your Frustration, REGAIN Control Of Your Finances and NEVER Have To Worry Again ($9.99)

In times like these you absolutely must have control over your portfolio. Retirees are scared. They do not know what to do with their investments. It does not have to stay that way. I reveal an entirely new approach to investing that can give retirees renewed confidence that all is not lost, that there is a better approach which can give them what they need, and the assurance they needto feel comfortable and confident—perhaps for the first time ever.

I begin by giving you an insiders' understanding of the Wall Street System. Make no mistake, this is still very much a system where the buyer needs to be aware and that's what I'm going to do: make you aware. But, I do not stop there. Further chapters reveal an approach to investing based on modeling the traits used by some of the most successful investors around. What is so exciting, though, is that a lot of the people I'm referring to are just like you--people who have successfully applied these traits to their own situation with tremendous results.

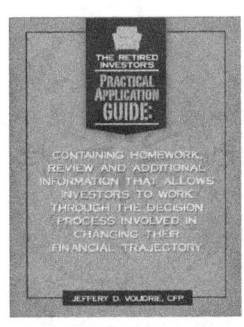

How Successful Investors Tripled The Return of the S&P 500: The Practical Application Guide

The free companion study guide to *How Successful Investors Tripled The Return of the S&P 500: The SECRET to Stop Playing By Wall Street's Rules, End Your Frustration, REGAIN Control Of Your Finances and NEVER Have To Worry Again*

Annuity Alert: Beware Of The Allianz Masterdex 10® ($9.99)

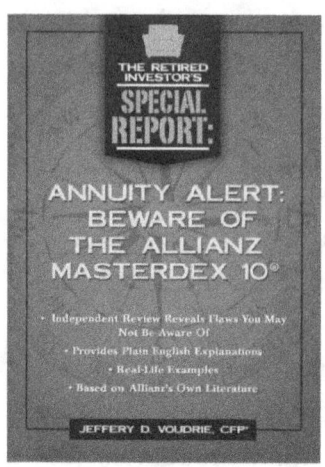

Everyone should be fully informed before they make any investment decision. By "fully informed," I mean having gathered opinions both for and against. This is a biased report. I don't like the MasterDex 10 TM. My purpose here is to tell why the MasterDex 10TM may not be what you are looking for.

That's not the insurance company's responsibility. I see it as mine. In this report, I use the company's own sales literature about its product as a reference point, and then I further detail my point by explaining what is outlined in the company's "Statement of Understanding."

As with most contractual language, the Statement of Understanding may be difficult to understand, even for a financial advisor. That's why I try to explain everything in terms that you may be more familiar with.

Steve Dinnen, financial columnist for *The Des Moines Register*, calls me "a lone voice in the wilderness" when it comes to speaking out on the downside of equity-indexed annuities, and that's precisely what I do here – speak out. Loudly and strongly! As a nationallysyndicated columnist, I have the opportunity to speak my mind about investing to a large number of readers each week. I don't pull any punches with them, and I won't pull any punches with you.

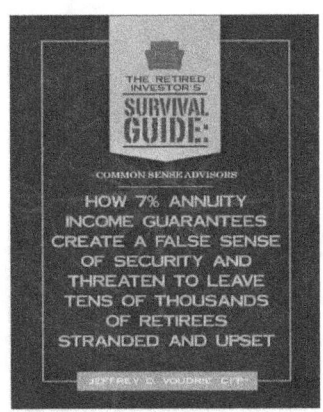

The 7% Annuity Income Guarantee Exposed

How 7% Annuity Income Guarantees Create A False Sense Of Security And Threaten To Leave Tens Of Thousands Of Retirees Stranded And Upset ($9.99)

Annuity salespeople certainly know how to deliver a persuasive sales pitch. But this report is designed to give you the otherside of the variable annuity story. Our viewpoint is unique and quite frankly, goes against the industry grain. Granted, many respected advisors firmly believe that variable annuities are good for consumers. But our opinion is quite different. In the end, only you can decide what is best for your situation. But if you don't know all the facts, how can you make an informed decision?

I'm going to give you facts you can't readily find anywhere else, certainly not from the advisors that sell variable annuities. Once you've read this report, you will no longer be an easy mark for commission-hungry advisors. And you will discover better ways to invest that will put you in control of your financial future and get you ahead of the game in the long haul.

Introduction

What would happen if you suddenly had to adjust your lifestyle DOWN by 25%? How would your survive? What would you have to give up?

If you are in or near retirement, your ability to maintain your standard of living is in jeopardy. As Americans, we face serious and growing threats to our way of life. Based on my analysis, I believe that there will be millions of American retirees who will have to dramatically change their lifestyle—and I don't want you to be one of them.

Our once-great nation is struggling. Washington has been mired in political gridlock for years and there doesn't seem to be any viable solution in sight. Despite what people in Washington want us to think, we realize that our economy isn't doing as well as it should. People can't find work. If we used the same formula for the "Misery Index" as was used in the 1970s, it is lower now than when Jimmy Carter was President.

For most of my lifetime, the United States of America has been the greatest country in the world. The US Dollar has enjoyed "reserve currency" status. That meant that virtually all the trade around the globe had to occur in US Dollars. Now, there is a real and present danger that the US Dollar will lose that reserve status in the next decade—if not sooner. If history is any guide, the impact on our economy and your standard of living will be significant.

That's why it is so important that you take a more active role in how your investments are managed. As I write this in late 2014, the U.S. stock market continues to set all-time highs, yet very few retirees are participating in that growth because they left the market after suffering horrendous losses in the 2008 crash.

Despite what the financial media and the Wall Street System wants us to believe, that everything is fine, we realize that we are in a precarious position. We've experienced the Tech Bubble in 1999 and saw it burst from 2000 to 2003. We endured the Housing Bubble pop in 2008, and the signs we see today are telling us that the bubble we are in now may be even worse.

I believe that conditions are ripe for another major stock market correction or crash. We all intuitively know it is coming, we just don't know exactly when. If you are invested with a traditional advisor and follow the Wall Street System's advice, then you are at risk. If you are invested the same way as everyone else, then you are part of a massive herd, and when the correction or crash happens, you will get slaughtered like everyone else.

It doesn't have to be that way.

I want to give you the information that you need to avoid it. It starts by educating yourself, by realizing that much of what is put forth by the financial services industry is designed to benefit <u>them, not you</u>. In other words, you need to understand how this industry works so you can more effectively gauge whether its advice is really in your best interest.

That is the purpose of this book: it serves as a primer on the different type of income-oriented investments and those that sell them.

The Help You Need in Today's Economic Climate:

Can you earn the income in retirement that you need in today's sluggish economy, with historically low interest rates? Why hasn't the financial services industry helped more than to say, "Times are tough"? Can you still create an income that you can retire on without having to continue working, as so many do in 21st-Century America?

If you are going to successfully navigate today's uncertain and turbulent economic waters, you are going to need help, special help, very personalized help. Read on.

This book will examine the questions above and many others as it offers reasons for optimism in today's uncertain financial climate—if you are willing to acknowledge that times have radically changed and you will need to as well. These pages will demonstrate why simply turning your money over to a financial "expert" is the wrong choice and how you can take advantage of a new type of private, personal money manager.

To answer the first question above, YES, you can earn the income in retirement that you need, but you must put your money in the right places. In today's volatile markets you have to find a money manager that is nimble and instantly reactive to market fluctuations.

Everything moves faster these days, from information to market swings. This book will offer wise counsel on investing your precious dollars in this current epoch.

Initially we will examine the keys to getting the retirement income you need, then look closely at the differences between traditional financial advisors and new-era private, personal money managers. In conclusion I will give you trustworthy advice on how to make sure that your money is safe in today's turbulent economic environment, so that you can avoid any large losses that you might have experienced in the past decade or so.

Why listen to me? Because I am an advisor, aCertified Financial Planning Professional® with more than20years of experience and the author of the syndicated financial advice column "Guarding Your Wealth." I've been interviewed by major newspapers such as *The Wall Street Journal* and have appeared on national TV. I have three U.S. patents on the systems and processes that I've designed, which allow me to effectively manage my clients' investments. I began with Edward Jones in 1986 and have worked as a broker for a regional bank, but none of these positions gave me the freedom to pursue non-traditional ways of helping my clients, so I started my own firm in 2001.

More important than all of these credentials is the fact that I have worked with many people who are retired or near-retired, and I helped them plot a successful course through the market crashes of 2001 and 2008. I've also helped scores of nervous investors preserve, grow and protect their wealth.

The Type of People I Want to Help

Before I unpack the three keys to successfully navigating your way through the current economy, let me further establish my credibility by demonstrating that I understand *you,* the anxious investor:

- You worked long and hard to get to where you are today.

- You are rational and realize that in most areas of life there aren't any shortcuts.
- You have not bought into the television commercials about getting rich through real estate, working at home a few hours a day (love those commercials with the guy in a hot tub surrounded by beautiful women and drinking champagne—pure fantasy!) or grabbing a government handout.

No, you have EARNED every dollar you've been able to save. You've earned it by working hard day in and day out. You've earned it by going to work every day and doing your best. You've earned it by being frugal—you've lived *beneath* your means.

You probably didn't have the biggest house on the block or a new car every two years when you were in your 30s. You weren't going on expensive vacations and didn't have "vacation homes" when you were in your 40s. You probably drove cars until they fell apart. Most of you probably lived in the same home for a decade or more.

With all that in mind, let's be honest: you know that wealth doesn't just *magically appear*—it's takes **hard work, sacrifice** and **patience.** Am I right?

I'm also going to bet that you are concerned about our country and the direction it's going in. We all grew up knowing that America was THE greatest place on earth. It was a land of opportunity and freedom, a place where you could work hard, support a family and build wealth.

It didn't matter if you were a penniless, first-generation immigrant in New York or a couple in the Midwest just struggling to get by. We all had the opportunity to succeed, and the system was set up to help us do it.

Now all that seems to have changed. While *you've* lived within your means, the government has been wildly spending, and frankly it is putting the financial viability of our nation at risk. Most Americans think the best days of our country are behind us.

And, I'll wager that you are concerned that your children—and your grandchildren--aren't going to have the opportunities that you had.

Finally, I'll guess that you are also probably more concerned about your financial situation <u>now</u> than you have been in decades.

Wisdom from the Past No Longer Works Today

In the past (and even now), you may have followed Wall Street's "wisdom" that you should invest your money in stocks and bonds for the longterm, using a strategy referred to as "Buy and Hold." An advisor used pretty charts that showed the performance of the stock market over the past 100 years and, sure enough, it looked like it went from the lower left corner to the upper right corner.

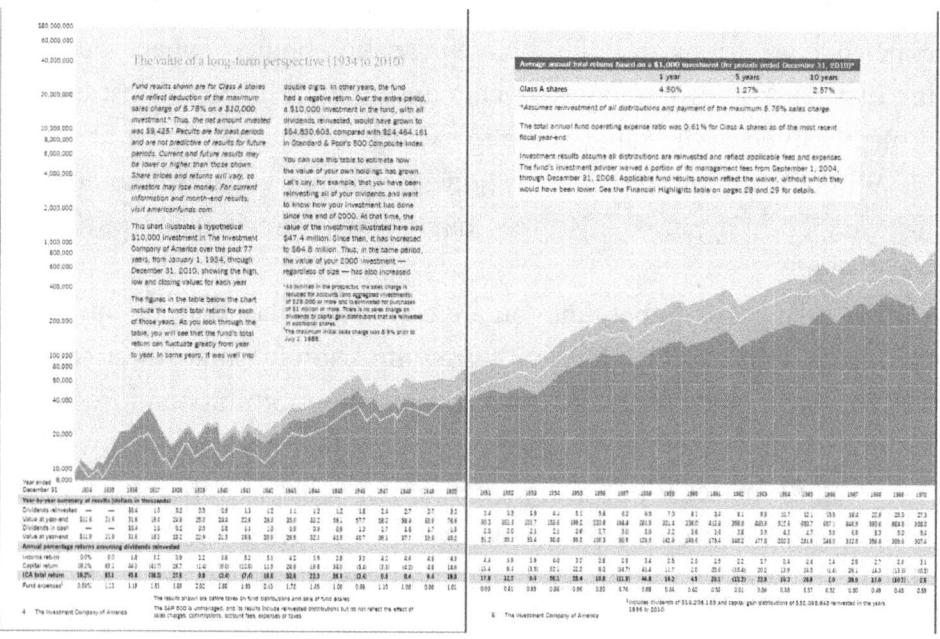

The Retired Investor's Survival Guide

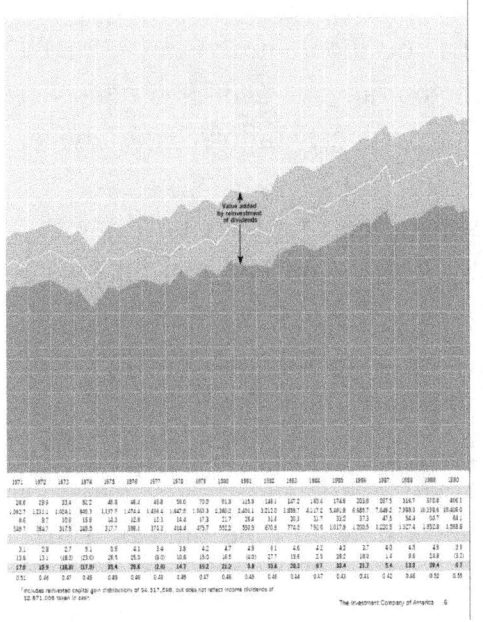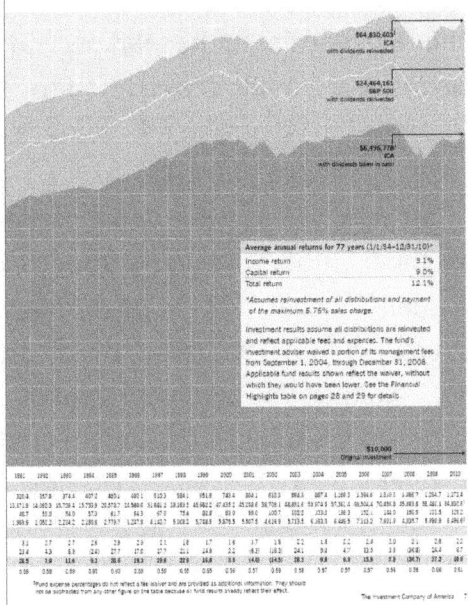

This "strategy" sounded reasonable because it made sense that it would be hard to "time the market." If you initially invested when the markets were in a general uptrend, such as the period between 2003 and 2007, then you probably felt pretty good and thought that this investing strategy was working. Some declines made you feel uncomfortable when your retirement account dropped 7-10%, but you were able to persevere. During that time period, the market continued to set higher lows and higher highs—it was trending up.

On July 13th, 2007, the S&P 500 hit an all-time high of 1552. Finally, it surpassed the previous high of 1527 that was set on March 24th in 2000! Even if you had purchased your mutual fund back in 2000 you were finally back to where you started. "See, holding on was the right thing to do," you told yourself. But then, the picture started to change.

The Credit Crisis began in the summer of 2007. In the last two weeks of July 2007, the S&P 500 dropped around 7.7%, ending at 1433 on August 3rd. That's a pretty big decline in two weeks! You were probably a little concerned; this seemed a little different than previous declines, so you called your advisor. You were told not to worry, that this was normal in the markets and that you should just "hang in there" and that it would recover. You trusted your advisor and knew s/he was "trained" in what s/he was doing, so you nervously followed the advice. And, it worked out well.

The market turned around and started heading back up. By early October 2007 you had earned back all that you had lost and were actually ahead! "I'm so glad I hung in there," you thought. "Look how much I would have lost if I had sold back in early August like I wanted to." Neither you nor your broker stopped to think that a market that dropped so quickly, then recovered just as quickly, might be a sign of danger ahead.

On October 12th, the S&P 500 set a new all-time high of 1561. "See, the credit crisis wasn't as bad as we thought." Wrong!

By November 23rd the S&P 500 had dropped 7.75% again. In a period of four months the market had set two highs and, both times, plunged more than 7% afterward. The last "recovery" had conditioned you to sit still because you <u>knew</u> it would come back. Besides, your advisor told you everything was okay and it started to look that way because the market would head back up for a few weeks, only to drop down further than it did the previous time. Now the market was establishing a pattern of *lower* lows and *lower* highs.

After the S&P 500 set its high of 1561 in 2007, it plunged to an intra-day low in March 2009 of 640. That's a top-to-bottom crash of 59%!

Now, in late 2014 as I write, the average has gotten a little shakier, despite its new all-time highs, dropping in mid-October at a rate unseen over three days since 2011, settling in at 1874. Are the days of crashes behind us? Is it smooth sailing ahead? Is it time to move more and more money out of bonds and into stocks? Are dividend stocks something I should be looking at? These are all questions that you are probably asking.

At some point you probably threw in the towel during the zigzag pattern at the end of the last decade. I bet there were many times during that period that you *wanted* your advisor to do something. You probably tried earnestly to explain your concerns, but each time you reminded yourself that the advisor was a trained professional that knew more about investing than you did, so you gritted your teeth and did what s/he suggested. And, you paid the price.

Some of you saw the value of your investments drop 30-50% or more during those years, and now you are devastated and scared. You absolutely can't afford to suffer any additional losses of any size. Your margin for error is small, your safety cushion is gone. It will take all you have left and then some to meet your needs.

Some of you may have been forced back to work. Others among you probably have to work years longer than you planned. You are confused and don't know what to do. You followed the professionals' advice and what happened? You have concluded that you shouldn't have invested in stocks in the first place.

Now, you optimistically think that there has to be something out there that you can invest in that will allow you to start recovering from your losses without all the risk. You hope there is; you desperately want there to be. You are searching.

Can You Trust the Latest Advice from the Self-Proclaimed Experts?

You've attended free seminars and met with different advisors, and it seems as if all of them are proposing a new kind of annuity product.

For example, there is the fixed index annuity (sometimes referred to as an equity-indexed annuity). The way you understand it, there's no way you can lose money--they guarantee it! The value of your account won't drop in the years the stock market goes down, yet you'll get to participate in the gains when it goes up. That's exactly what you've been looking for!

Another advisor has suggested a variable annuity, which you may have owned in the past. In fact, it could have been the investment you had when you lost all that money! However, these "new" variable annuities are different; they have riders that guarantee you'll earn at least 7% a year for the rest of your life. Wow! It seems as if your biggest decision is whether you want the "fixed index" or the "variable" version.

Except...except for that nagging feeling in the pit of your stomach that these sound almost too good, *certainly* too good to be true. There is just something about them that doesn't feel right.

So, you're hesitant to take action. <u>You should be</u>.

Not everyone you talk to is pitching these annuities. There are some advisors that are suggesting more traditional investments, such as muni-bonds. They tell you these bonds are safe because the government can always raise taxes to pay them off. They don't fluctuate like the stock market, so you know you'll get your money back when they mature.

Or maybe the advisors around you are suggesting dividend-paying stocks. You can earn a much higher yield with them than you can in a Certificate of Deposit and there's little chance that a company like AT&T is going to go bankrupt.

Some brave (or foolish) advisors may be recommending that you spread your money between various mutual funds and follow the same strategy that got you in so much trouble the last time, but this time it's different, they claim.

Now you are even more confused. All the advisors you talked to seemed honest and sincere. They've been advisors for several years so they must know what they're doing. What makes it so confusing for you is that each advisor is telling you that all the other advisors are wrong and their whiz-bang product is THE answer. It's enough to make you want to throw your money in the bank and do nothing--but there are a lot of banks that seem to be in trouble too!

What are you to going to do?

That's what I want to talk about in this book.

I will expose the hidden dangers inherent in most fixed index annuities in a summary of a book that I have done. Based on the emails

I have received from grateful readers, this book has saved thousands of people from making a decision they would soon live to regret.

I will also share a condensed version of my report on variable annuities that goes into great detail to explain how each of the guarantees and features *really* work, and the practical impact they have on the investor. You will see that the "guarantees" will rarely do what the investor thinks they will.

I also will share a synopsis of my report that helps people just like you know whether or not you even need an advisor, and if so, what you should look for in one.

All of this information is designed to help the individual investor learn what the advisor isn't telling them. I believe that the financial services industry often (knowingly or unknowingly) takes advantage of the little guy. To Wall Street, someone with $250,000 or $600,000 or even $1,000,000 is a "little guy." That's why I think it's VITAL that investors like you take steps to defend yourself. If you don't, you can be easy prey.

You'll find that what I recommend is probably far different than the advice of anyone else you've talked with. My philosophy is different and my approach is different.

Before I get into that, though, we need to step back and look at the bigger picture. In order for you to start heading down the right path, I believe you need to know that there is hope.

What You Need to Change

If you are going to earn the retirement income you need in this unpredictable age, you are going to have to change your expectations, your mindset and your approach to investing. Let's look at each of these.

The Three Keys to Getting the Retirement Income You Need

I can summarize my popular and insightful approach to investing by highlighting these three keys, all of which you will need to turn to unlock the wealth that you need for retirement:

1. Change the way you view and work with an advisor.
2. Hire a qualified professional but retain full control as you invest on your own.
3. Learn the advantages and disadvantages of the different income-oriented investments so you can decide which is right for you.

If I had to summarize my advice in a nutshell, it would be this: the key to getting the income that you need in today's low-interest-rate environment is not to find a new type of investment, but to find traditional investments that offer the best opportunity, then *manage them correctly*. It is that last part—"manage them correctly"—where most people and advisors go wrong and live to regret it. I want to help you know how you can more effectively manage those investments regardless of whether you do it on your own or with the help of a professional.

The Critical Importance of Attitude

Your attitude has a major impact on how you invest and the results you receive. You've had a difficult few years in the markets. The combination of losing money and economic, political and global uncertainty is enough to cause anyone to be depressed. Perhaps you've failed to participate in the recent market recovery because you didn't think it was "real." It's as if a dark cloud is hanging over us and we can't see how things will ever get better. If you are like many of the investors I talk to, you have a negative attitude.

In order to successfully invest for income in today's low-interest-rate environment, the first thing that has to change is your attitude. Everything is not doom and gloom. There is hope.

Our tendency as humans is to look at our current situation and project the same circumstances long into our future. For instance, if things are going well today, we think they'll continue to go well for the foreseeable future. If we earn 10% on our investments this year, we think we'll earn close to that for many years. Likewise, if we lose 10% this year we also project to lose 10% a year into the future. Neither is true.

Our attitude is crucial because it will affect the types of investments we buy and when we buy them. It causes us to be biased, and when we are biased we tend to view events that occur through the lens of our attitude. Psychologists refer to this as "confirmation bias."

For instance, if I think that our country is in trouble and that our economy isn't going to recover anytime soon, then I will tend to give more credence to information and data points that confirm that opinion and less to those that don't. If a consumer sentiment report shows a lower number than expected, I may weight that as being more important than the fact that the stock market has been going up the last few weeks. Beware of confirmation bias.

As a country, the very core of who we are is being challenged, and to many the future looks bleak. It's easy to think America's best days are behind her and to feel depressed and afraid.

There is a quote from the movie *"Tora! Tora! Tora!"* that comes to mind when I think about what is going on in our country. Japanese Admiral Yamamoto said at the end of the Pearl Harbor attack, *"I fear all we have done is to awaken a sleeping giant and fill him with a terrible resolve."* Yamamoto had seen firsthand the power of America's factories and people, and feared that instead of inflicting a winning blow, the attack had simply awakened a sleeping giant. And, as we know from history, that's exactly what happened.

I believe that we are witnessing the awakening of the American "sleeping giant" once again. It seems that for years Washington has been immune to the needs of its people. As voters, we felt powerless and frustrated, without any real hope that we make a real difference.

All that is changing. People are mad. They are fed up. We are seeing in election after election that voters are resolved to "take back our country" and to change the downward trajectory of this great nation. This fight isn't about Democrat versus Republican. It's about those who are fiscally conservative versus those who are not.

Regardless of who is in control of our government, it will take years to turn the economy around, but I believe that we can and will do that.

So, now is *not* the time to feel discouraged or depressed. We are a great nation filled with hard-working, creative, productive, entrepreneurial people. We are the land of opportunity. More importantly, we are a people of action, and thankfully we have a form of government which must act in response to the actions of its people.

Are we living in tough financial times now? Yes. Is our economy struggling? Yes. Are you going to have to make hard lifestyle choices to allow you to get through this? In some cases, yes, but making the proper investment choices requires a more balanced attitude. We need to focus more on the facts—prices and market statistics—than on emotions.

I'm a money manager and my clients pay me to take the actions necessary to protect the value of their accounts and to make them grow. Therefore, it's vital that I take into account a wide variety of market barometers and weight them appropriately. It's essential that I not let my attitude or emotions bias my decisions.

It is highly likely that you, too, need to clear away a bad attitude and negative emotions. You might need to change your expectations, your mindset and your approach as well. I'm going to talk about all three of these factors and then get into more specifics about how you can invest in this environment.

You Must Change Your Expectations

The environment we live in now is considerably different than the one we have been in for the past 20+ years. That means we must adjust our expectations. Otherwise, you will find yourself unable to get the returns you need and/or unable to take more risk to try to get them.

Historically, we were toldthat we should expect conservative portfolios to earn 5-7% each year and growth-oriented portfolios to "average" 10% a year. Every financial planner or advisor would project 10% as the long-term average return on your investments. At that rate, you had a comfortable cushion so that you could retire early and not have to worry.

Times have changed, however, and I decided to develop an innovative tool that allows me to stress-test a person's retirement income plan and determine the probability of success under myriad conditions. Those that have been through this process have come away with an in-depth understanding of the strengths and weaknesses in the current plan and the action they should take based on the types of scenarios we might encounter over the next several years.

For instance, here is what the probability of success looks like when you use the traditional assumptions that have been made by financial planners over the past decade:

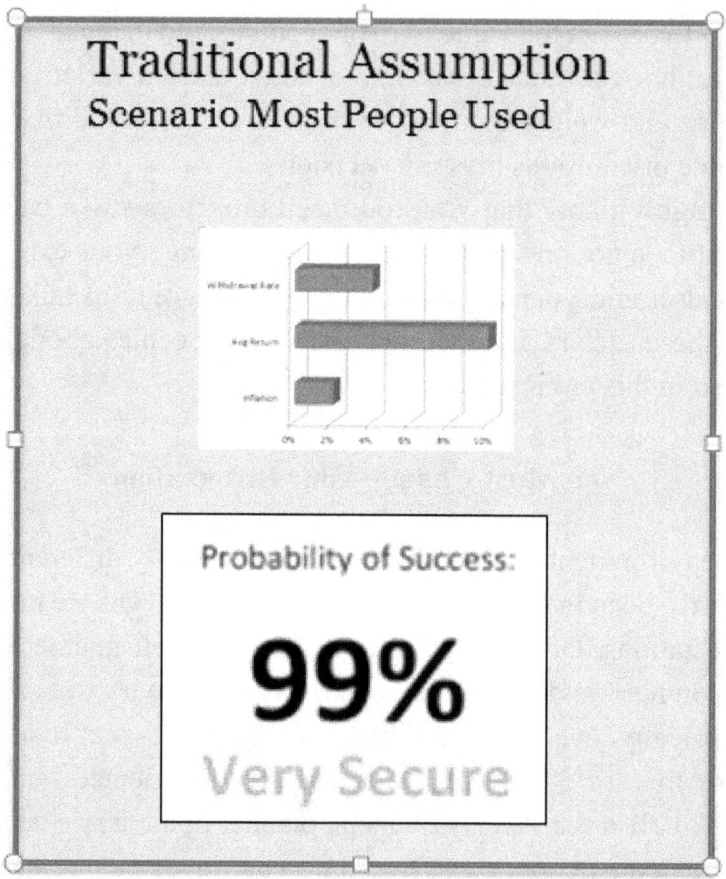

The bar graph above is based on a 10% return, withdrawal rates of 4% and inflation at 1%--the very conditions that many of today's retirees based their future plans on. However, when these assumptions are adjusted to more accurately reflect what we have experienced in the past five years, we see a startling forecast:

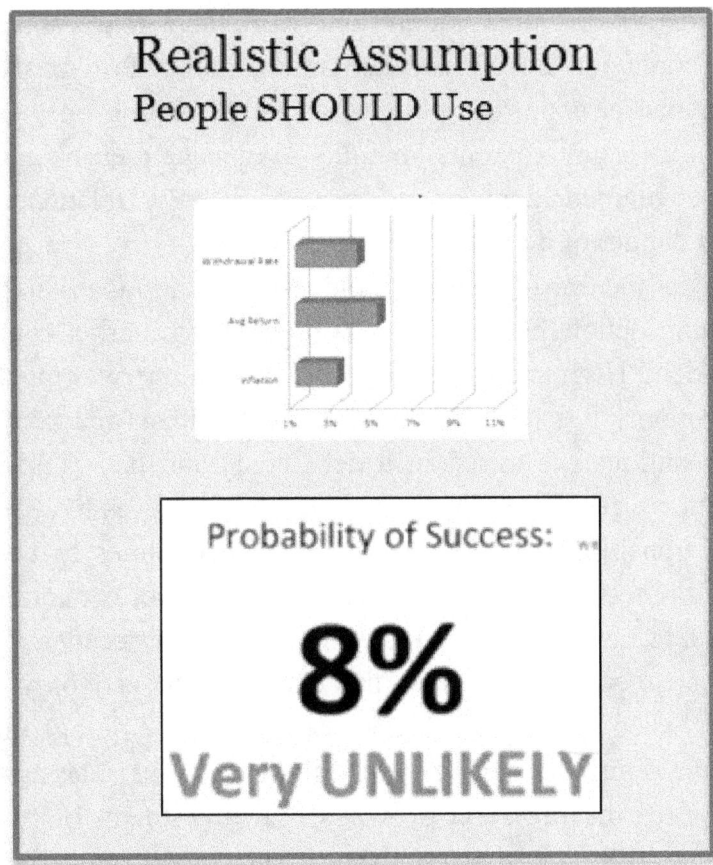

This second bar graph is based on conditions more prevalent in today's zero interest rate policy (ZIRP) environment—5% average annual return, inflation between 2% and 3% and the traditional 4% withdrawal rate.

In conditions like these, many retirees have become more concerned about the likelihood that they will run out of money within their lifetime. The probabilities from this retirement income plan stress test indicate that those concerns are not only justified, but that many retirees need to take action <u>now</u>.

Traditionally rosy projections such as the one in the first bar graph no longer fit today's financial world. We are seeing tremendous upheaval in the global financial system, and some of the biggest financial institutions inour country and worldhave gone bankrupt. The financial contagion has spread across the globe. Previously, small, emerging market countries were at risk of defaulting on their bonds because of their governments' inability to manage their balance sheet. Now, it's developed countries such as Greece, Italy, Ireland, and Spain that are in danger of default.

The first- and third-largest economies (U.S. and Japan) in the world have soaring deficits and must rely on emerging market countries to buy their debt. High unemployment and uncertainty over the direction of our economy has reduced our demand for items made by China. European nations are mired in a debt crisis and have implemented austerity measures that will impede growth. Countries like China and India are transitioning from export-driven economies to economies fueled by domestic consumption. There is a shift of economic power (from West to East) underway thatwill continue for decades.

Compare certain aspects of the current U.S. economy with its portrait between 1990 and 2010. Interest rates have plunged from the high double digits to nearly zero. Retirement plans such as 401(k)'s used to be all the rage and provoked the investment of billions of dollars in equities. The advent of the personal computer and the Internet revolutionized business and resulted in tremendous productivity gains. The end result was huge amounts of money flowing into the U.S. stock markets.

Those days are over. I don't believe that we will see returns anywhere near the "historic"10% average for many, many years. There may be a good year here or there, but we aren't going to average 10% a year for the next 10 years in the stock market. With high unemployment and a sluggish economy, we aren't going to see interest rates in the 5-7% range anytime soon either. I think that interest rates will go up, but they might not increase right away.

Japan embarked on quantitative easing in the '80s and has seen interest rates near 0% for more than a decade. The 30-year U.S. Treasury Bond is currently yielding 3.23% while the equivalent 30-

year Japanese government bond yields 1.79%!Recently, Japan decided to double-down by devaluing its currency significantly in hopes of spurring inflation and its economy. So far it hasn't worked. The truth is: <u>there's no way to know for sure whether any government's actions to control its economy will be successful</u>. That's life in our new era.

The main point here is that I don't expect the interest rate environment to be conducive to earning 3-5% a year in ultra-safe Certificates of Deposit nor U.S. government bonds anytime soon. U.S. equity markets will not provide a relatively stable place to average 10% a year. All of this means that you need to change your expectations. Look at your ability to retire or your ability to stay retired with the assumption that you will only earn 3-5% year.

Living on an income base earning 3-5% annually is going to require many of you who are retired or near retirement to make major lifestyle changes. For some, it's going to require you to work longer, perhaps several years longer. It may force others to go back to work. People are going to have to adjust their lifestyles to lower their standard of living—they will *have* to downsize.

Americans are not used to lowering their standard of living because few have had to do it in the past 25 years. Successfully navigating through financial hardship requires very tough choices. It may mean selling your home and keeping your vehicles longer. It may mean forgoing the annual or semi-annual vacation.

If I am even partially correct, these sorts of lifestyle changes will have a further negative impact on our economy. It will result in less spending at the very time our economy needs more spending. Those in their 50s will continue to work longer, and experienced retirees re-entering the workforce will result in fewer job openings for the younger generation. This demographic shift will have ripple effects throughout our economy and for export countries around the world.

There is more risk in assuming you are able to earn 8-10% a year and basing your lifestyle on that than there is in preparing now for much lower returns. It's also going to be to your advantage to make these adjustments before your friends and neighbors do.(Do you have friends and/or children that could be significantly affected should these events play out? You might consider sharing this bookwith them so they can make similar changes in their lifestyle.)

How Much Do You Need To Earn?

We just talked about preparing for lower interest rates, but how can you know how much you need to earn to sustain your lifestyle? Before I conclude this section, let me walk you through the steps needed to find your required rate of return. For now, let's just calculate a rough estimate. Based on that we can then drill down and fine tune if needed.

Step 1: Determine how much it currently takes you to live on, assuming that you maintain your lifestyle.

Step 2: Calculate the total amount of assets you have available to invest for income.

Step 3: Determine if you are willing to use principal to meet your needs. Depending on the result of step 4, you will have to decide between lowering your standard of living and preserving principal or maintaining your standard of living and invading principal.

Step 4: Find an online calculator that will tell you how long your money will last.You will need to experiment with different input variables such as assumed interest rate, annual rate of increase in withdrawals (to take into account inflation) and tax rates (assume they'll go up!)

Step 5: Add the number of years the calculator says your money will last to the age of the youngest spouse and see if you are confident that your money will last longer than you do. For instance, let's say the calculator predicts that your money will last 23 years. If one spouse is 65 and one is 71, add 23+65=88. Ask yourself: "Do I think that I will live that long?" If not, are you willing to bet your lifestyle on it?

Step 6: Re-run the calculation using lower assumed rates of return (or lower withdrawals or both) until you get a number of years that you feel comfortable with.

Step 7: You should end up with an assumed rate of return and a withdrawal amount. How much does this differ from what you are currently taking from your investments? If it's less than you are currently taking, and all that you are dipping into is interest--congratulations! If it's more than you are currently earning on your investments, then you need to sit down and try to see what you can adjust in your lifestyle in order to get by on that amount. What you change will depend on your priorities. (Note: if you'd like to save yourself the time needed for the above calculations and receive a much more thorough analysis, ask me about my Retirement Income Stress Test.)

There are a few points you need to keep in mind during this exercise. First, take the results of the calculator with a grain of salt. It assumes that you will earn the same rate of return every year and take out the same amount. You won't. Investment returns vary, even if you aren't investing in the stock market. There's no way to know what interest rates are going to be in the future. On the one hand, you probably don't want to assume that interest rates will remain at 0% for 20 years, nor should you assume they'll be 10%. (My sophisticated Stress Test models variable returns each year.)

Second, your circumstances are going to change. That's one of the problems I have with the "comprehensive financial plans" done by many firms. You walk in, answer their questions and they print out a boatload of charts, graphs and numbers, and all of them are out of date by the time you walk out of their office! The likelihood of real life matching the assumptions of the plan is very small.

I approach financial planning from a more practical perspective. You can run the numbers in the calculator that seem reasonable today, but you will want to re-run the numbers every so often so that they take into account the real changes in the value of your investments.

For instance, based on the estimates above, you may not need to adjust your current lifestyle. If you are assuming a 7% interest rate, though, and your actual interest rate (earnings) six months from now are only 2%, then it's unlikely you will earn the full 7% for the year. You might plug in 4% into the calculator to see how it influences your long-term outlook. Obviously, you shouldn't make drastic lifestyle changes based on what has occurred in the past six months, but running the numbers helps underscore the importance that return will play in your long-term plans.

If you see that your actual return continues to deviate from your projected returns for 12 – 18 months or longer, then it may be time to think seriously about adjusting your spending or how you are invested.

Conversely, there may be something in your situation that dramatically affects your spending, such as increased medical costs or unforeseen home repairs. The expense side of the equation can affect your long-term projections just as much as the rate of return on your investments. Typically, both the income and expenses are going to change over time, so continue to go through the exercise every 6-12 months. Understanding the impact that deviations have on the sustainability of your lifestyle will allow you to more effectively manage your investments.

One more issue needs to be addressed if you are to successfully pilot your retirement income plan: there is no way to determine what type of scenario we will face in the future, no matter what the "experts" on TV say. We also cannot predict how long each set of conditions will last and what set will follow them.

For example, we have been in a low-interest-rate/slow-growth environment where assets like homes have been deflating in value. We might transition to a rising-interest-rate/slow-growth era, but we can't know for sure. We also cannot predict how long such an environment will endure or what will follow it.

Why is this crucial? Because the type of environment that predominates determines the type of investments you should use. Each investment type performs differently in differing contexts. The absolute keys to success are: 1) correctly identifying the type of environment that exists, and, 2) using the investments that perform best in that specific environment. My Stress Test is based on these keys, which few financial planners consider.

To summarize, it is vital that you change your expectations about a realistic annual return and adjust your lifestyle accordingly. Use handy calculators to help you project how long your money will last. Instead of assuming a traditional interest rate of 8-10%, use a return that better reflects the realities of the new economy: 3-5%. Your money won't last nearly as long using this more likely interest rate and you may need to downsize as a result.

If you need to make adjustments, you should do it sooner rather than later. Understanding the impact that your expenses and rate earned on your investments have on your lifestyle will allow you to more effectively manage your investments and feel more in control.

You Must Change Your Mind-set

Successfully investing for income in an uncertain-interest-rate environment requires the proper mind-set. There is a dangerous perspective that retirees often have that opens them up to being taken advantage of by the financial services industry: the "set-it-and-forget-it" approach to investment. Unless that mind-set is changed, you can easily make a mistake that you will regret for years.

Beware of any magic product that will guarantee your future so that you don't have to worry about what happens in the stock market or with interest rates. Savvy salespeople know that most people don't like dealing with financial decisionsnorhaving to decide how their money should be invested.

Those with this "set-it-and-forget-it" mind-set, though, think that all they have to do is find a packaged product like an annuity and then they won't have to deal with it for another 10-30 years. Typically, however, events will *not* unfold as planned.

Those with this mind-set are looking for a sense of security, but what they don't realize (and won't find out until it's too late) is that all they are getting is a FALSE sense of security. In many cases, reality won't set in until years later, and by then it will be too late. It's awfully dangerous, in my opinion, to trust something as important as your lifestyle to a one-size-fits-all product, especially when you can't change your mind without losing tens of thousands of dollars.

Ron Popeil made a fortune by selling products on infomercials. One of his most successful offerings was the Ronco ShowtimeRotisserie oven with the magic knob on the side. Whatever you put inside the oven, you would just turn the knob, "set it and forget it," and the result was perfectly cooked meat every time. I don't know how well "set it and forget it" works when you're cooking, but I know it doesn't work well at all when it comes to investing. Nevertheless, many people are constantly trying to find an investment that they can just set and forget.

The first step in changing your mind-set is understanding why you have it. Based on my conversations with thousands of investors over the years, I think people have certain mind-sets because they feel insecure making financial decisions and are afraid. They also have the mistaken impression that the advisor they are talking to knows more about managing money than they do.

Let's look at why people feel insecure about making financial decisions:

1. Because they don't have to make big financial decisions on a regular basis. For instance, how often do you make a decision to buy or sell a house or car? For most people it's not too often.
2. They don't have an educational background in finance. They may be a trained engineer or teacher, so they are comfortable in that area of expertise, but they incorrectly assume that their lack of a finance degree means they aren't qualified to make financial decisions.
3. They are afraid of making the wrong decision because they recognize the impact that their decision can have on their lifestyle. They may also be afraid of having to go back to work,

orthey may be afraid of not having enough money to last the rest of their life. They may also be afraid of being a burden to their children.

These are ALL valid fears. They are normal and it's rational to have them.

The problem isn't that people are afraid; the problem is their reaction to it. Our natural tendency is to avoid dealing with the realities that make us afraid.

I believe that most times we need to trust our gut. We should have a peace about the decisions that we make, and my advice to investors is that if you don't feel at peace when making a decision, if there's something that doesn't feel right, then you need to get more information or keep looking until you do feel a sense of peace.

People with this fearful mindset also incorrectly assume the advisor they are talking to knows more about managing money than they do. I started in this industry in 1986 and I've seen what goes on behind the curtain. I've also talked to investor after investor who feels that they were taken advantage of by their advisor.

Just about every advisor you talk to *isn't* trained in how to *manage* money; they are trained in how to sell financial products. "Financial advisors" are salespeople. That's especially true if the advisor is recommending an insurance product such as an index or variable annuity; those products are almost always sold on commission.

Very few advisors manage money. They hand that responsibility off to someone else—either an insurance company, a mutual fund company or a private money manager. The traditional "advisor" will work with the client to allocate the money between different types of investments (cash, bonds, real estate, equities) and then further diversify the money within each type. Most firms subscribe to a research firm (Ibbotson) and utilize the allocations they provide. Other firms have research departments that create them internally.

The point is that the advisor isn't doing *anything* that you can't do just as easily on your own using free online tools. The advisor doesn't have inside information that allows them to better allocate your funds.

That's one thing that makes what I do so different. I've created patented software systems and proprietary strategies that aid me in the daily management of each client's account. Now, I spend my time doing what my clients expect of an advisor—I closely monitor the markets and their accounts, I adjust the strategies based on market and economic conditions, and I take action when necessary to protect the value of their accounts.

To summarize this section, I believe that people have a set-it-and-forget-it mind-set because they feel insecure in making financial decisions, because they are afraid, and because they have the mistaken impression that the advisor they are talking to knows more about managing money than they do.If you have this mind-set, you must change it.

Looking At Your Situation from a Different Perspective Can Help Correct Your Mind-Set

I've explained how most advisors know little about actually managing money. On the other hand, you know more than you think you do about managing money. You wouldn't be reading this report unless you had achieved a measure of wealth.

Think of how many years it took you to get to where you are today. Your current standingis the fruit of hundreds of decisions made over an extended period of time. For example, you made the choices to live within your means and to set money aside. It may not have always been that way. Early on you may have relied too much on credit. There are probably many decisions that you would have made differently were you to make them today. You've learned from your experiences, both good and bad. You had the ability to see those decisions play out over the years. That's wisdom.

Think about it! You didn't get to where you are today because of some get-rich-quick scheme. You had to be diligent. You had to make course corrections to adjust for changes in your situation and/or the world around you. These traits don't just apply to building wealth, they also apply to managing it.

There wasn't a magic pill you could take to become wealthy and there's not a magic investment that's going to allow you to set it and forget it. Is there any other area of your life, such as learning to shoot par on the golf course or advancing through the ranks at work or raising children, where you were able to just setitandforgetit?

If you can't set it and forget it in other areas of your life, why should you think that you can do that when it comes to managing your wealth? You shouldn't.

People often think their only option is to do everything themselves or to find a traditional advisor to do everything. That's not the case. There are a few new-era advisors that bridge this gap. Since they are so different from other advisors in the Wall Street System I am going to refer to this new breed as "private money managers."They recognize that for both parties to be successful, you have to stay in control and involved, yet that doesn't mean you have to pick every stock or bond or spend hours a day reading research. That's the private money manager's job. The investor and the private money managerdiscuss the direction you want to go in and strategies are suggested; the private money manager takes it from there.

Some clients email their private money manager several times a week and others have little contact with him/her. Either way, investors like you know that the private money manager has systems and processes in place to do what they expect. They find this to be incredibly refreshing compared to the frustrations inherent in working with a traditional advisor.

Finally, You Must Change Your Approach

Realize that no one is going to care as much about your money as you do.

The insurance company that handles that annuity doesn't care how much you make because it is virtually guaranteed to get its profit first. And, that company doesn't have to worry about you taking your money somewhere else, because if you do, the surrender penalties mean it only has to give you a portion of what you might have otherwise earned. Depending on when you pull your money out, you could get back LESS than what you put in! So, the insurance company definitely doesn't care as much as you do.

For example, let's say you put $500,000 into one popular indexed annuity I recently reviewed and the insurance company gave you a $50,000 bonus. If something happened and you needed to get your money back before the year was up, how much would you get? $437,500! That's a pretty good deal for the company, definitely not a good deal for you.

The traditional advisor doesn't care as much about your money as you do because you are just one of many clients that s/he has. If a broker working for a firm like Edward Jones has been in business for five years, then s/he should have more than 1,000 clients. Many brokers will have 2,000 clients. How much personal attention is your money going to get if you are one of 2,000 clients? Your money will get more of their attention if you're their largest client, but if you have that much money you shouldn't be working with them anyway!

Assuming there are 250 working days a year, the advisor would have to see four clients each day just to be able to see each one of them once in an entire year! When you work with a traditional advisor you'll be a small fish in a big pond. The advisor isn't going to care about your money as much as you do.

You might choose to invest on your own and put your money into one or more mutual funds. That way you have a team of professionals watching over your money. The mutual fund company probably has tens of thousands of people invested in the funds they manage. They don't know you from Adam...or Eve. Moreover, your money is lumped together into a big pool. If other investors put a lot of money into the pool it can hurt your return. If other investors pull their money out it can hurt your returns because the money manager could be forced into selling positions just to fund redemptions.

You are a minnow in the ocean when you invest using a mutual fund. That doesn't mean you shouldn't use a mutual fund, but you have to keep in mind that the mutual fund managers care even less about your money than the traditional advisor!

You may be surprised to hear this, but it's true: even when you become a client of a new-era private money manager, s/he is not going to care as much about your money as you do. The private money manager takes his/her responsibility to each client very seriously, and s/he only serves a very small number of clients, so each one is important to his/her financial success.

A private money manager is a boutique money manager that doesn't expect to EVER have 1,000 clients, or even 500 clients. S/he doesn't gauge success based on the number of clients s/he has—that's not thefocus.

The focus is on managing each client's money the best way s/he can and on giving them the attention they desire. With hours spent each day doing research and monitoring the markets, that's a full-time responsibility. Even though each of the clients is a big fish in a small pond, the truth is that even a private money manager won't care as much about your money as you do.

You will ALWAYS care more about your money than someone else because it's you and your loved ones who will bear the consequences. You bear the ultimate responsibility for how well or poorly it is managed. You will be the one having to go back to work, if necessary.

That's why it is so important that you keep control over and access to your money. If you don't have control you can't make changes, and you can't adapt to the unexpected. And let's face it—there have been a lot of unexpected events the past decade. We've seen recessions, the burst of the housing bubble, the banking crisis, the debt crisis and now a currency and economic crisis.

Why should the next decade be any different? As a country we are going to have to deal with ballooning deficits, the viability of Social Security and Medicare, and the implementation of the Healthcare Affordability Act (Obamacare), among other looming factors. Thus, you need to guard your ability to control your investments because your financial future does depend on it.

Pre-packaged Investment Products Are NOT What They Seem

Index and variable annuities are popular right now and you've probably either attended or been invited to attend free luncheon and dinner seminars where you're told how the guarantees provided will give you the peace of mind that you won't lose money when the market goes down, plus you'll make money when it goes up. What could be better?

Invariably, these annuities have some form of an income guarantee. Some of them guarantee that your balance will increase by 7% a year before you start taking distributions, and then you'll be guaranteed to get distributions of 5% for life.

After hearing this pitch, you conclude, "Wow, I'm NOT guaranteed to make 7% a year in the stock market, and with this I'd make at least 7% in those years the stock market goes down and still make at least that when the markets go up---there's no way I can lose! This is the best investment ever. I just have to put whatever I want inside the oven, turn the little knob on the side and set it and forget it!"

The problem with this conclusion is confusing a *paper* return with an *actual* return. The return on a stock or mutual fund is real. It's yours.

You can access it. The 7% guarantee associated with annuities is a *paper* or *make-believe* value increase. It's *not* yours. You *can't* withdraw it. It only comes into play IF you take lifetime distributions.

And those 5% distributions? You probably think it means you earn a 5% return on your money. It doesn't. Notice they use the term "income stream," not "return." That's because only 1% of the payment might be "interest" you've earned, while the other 4% is a return of your principal. Let's say you give me $100,000 and I guarantee to pay you $5,000 for 20 years. Assuming the underlying investment doesn't earn any money, the money left after 20 years is $0. The insurance companies would call that a 5% income stream even though your actual return was 0%. Worse, you gave them free use of your money for 20 years!

Please re-read the preceding paragraph so that you understand what a "5% income stream" actually means.

The best way to analyze an annuity is to calculate the minimum guaranteed return you will earn using the worst case scenario. This alleviates any confusion over what you are being told you can expect and what you are guaranteed. The minimum guaranteed interest rate is set by each state. On some policies I've looked at, it is 1.5%. Even that is misleading, though. That doesn't mean that you are guaranteed to earn 1.5% per year on every dollar you put in. It means you earn the minimum guaranteed interest rate on 87.5% of what you put in. Read it yourself:

What is the Guaranteed Minimum Return?

When EIAs were first sold in the mid-1990s, the guaranteed minimum return was typically 90 percent of the premium paid at a 3 percent annual interest rate. More recently, in part because of changes to state insurance laws, the guaranteed minimum return is typically at least 87.5 percent of the premium paid at

1 to 3 percent interest. However, if you surrender your EIA early, you may have to pay a significant surrender charge and a 10 percent tax penalty that will reduce or eliminate any return.[1]

So, let's say you put in $100,000 and they generously "give" you a bonus of $10,000! You are NOT guaranteed to make 1.5% a year on the $110,000, and you are not guaranteed to make 1.5% on $100,000. You ARE guaranteed to make 1.5% on $87,500. Look how this works out over 10 years:

	Invested	GSV BOY	Interest 1.5%	GSV EOY
Year 1	$ 100,000	$ 87,500	$ 1,313	$ 88,813
Year 2	$ 100,000	$ 88,813	$ 1,332	$ 90,145
Year 3	$ 100,000	$ 90,145	$ 1,352	$ 91,497
Year 4	$ 100,000	$ 91,497	$ 1,372	$ 92,869
Year 5	$ 100,000	$ 92,869	$ 1,393	$ 94,262
Year 6	$ 100,000	$ 94,262	$ 1,414	$ 95,676
Year 7	$ 100,000	$ 95,676	$ 1,435	$ 97,111
Year 8	$ 100,000	$ 97,111	$ 1,457	$ 98,568
Year 9	$ 100,000	$ 98,568	$ 1,479	$ 100,047
Year 10	$ 100,000	$ 100,047	$ 1,501	$ 101,547

That's right! After 10 years you are "guaranteed" to earn only $1,547 more than you put in.

The guarantees benefit and income riders provided by annuities are based on certain requirements being met, and very few investors are apt to ever meet all of the requirements. Even if they do, the returns probably aren't going to be what they think they'll be.

---

1 http://www.finra.org/investors/protectyourself/investoralerts/ annuitiesandinsurance/p010614, retrieved 6/9/13

Before leaving the topic of annuities, I want to comment on the risk associated with investing in them. I believe that those considering annuities often incorrectly assess the true risk involved. They have experienced losses in equities and tend to focus on how annuities may prevent that in the future, while ignoring other risks that can be just as devastating, such as <u>surrender penalties</u>.

Most people dismiss the potential loss associated with the penalties because they think there is little chance they will ever pay them. They tell themselves, "I don't expect to start drawing on this money for 10 years, so the penalties won't apply to me." Yet the likelihood of keeping the same annuity for 10 years is very small. Why? <u>Because insurance companies are constantly coming out with newer and better products so the agents can talk you into switching from one annuity to another.</u> That protects the insurance company because they don't have to deliver on the promises on the surrendered annuity, and it will be years before the investor accrues any benefits in the new one. It's GREAT for the insurance company and great for the agent (they get another 7% of your money); it's not so great for the investor. Is this one of the best investments for retirees? No.

Thus, here are two ways in which your approach has to change: 1) to realize that no one is going to be as concerned about your money as you are, and, 2) that most packaged products, such as annuities and mutual funds, aren't what they seem to be. Third, you must recognize that all things considered, traditional investments are going to be the best instrument to use.

Beyond this book, I have written extensively about the dangers of prepackaged products. Check out my book on variable annuities, my specialreport on annuity income guarantees or my in-depth analysis of the Allianz Masterdex 10. I also have authored a special report on equity-indexed annuities that you might find helpful.

After you finish this book, browse through the titles and covers I have listed in the initial pages of this work and see which of my other reports or books will answer the questions that you have. As a rule of thumb, I have not been a huge fan of prepackaged financial products, for reasons that I explain in great detail. I trust that my years of research and experience will help you to make the right choices with your precious money and nest egg.

How and Why Traditional Investments Are the Right Choice in a Non-Traditional Era

Most of you have lost a large amount of money investing in stocks, bonds and real estate investment trusts over the years. You have to realize that the reason you lost money wasn't because of the <u>type</u> of investment that was used, but <u>the way those investments were managed</u> as we try to distinguish which are the best investments for retirees.

Let me tell a story to illustrate: Imagine planting corn one year in a garden, but planting it too late and not watering it enough in a drought year. How much corn do you think you will eat in the fall? Not much!

Was the problem that you planted corn instead of green beans? Of course not. It wasn't the corn seed's fault, it was the way that the seed was tended.

It is the same way with investments. If you buy IBM stock late in the "season" after it had already gone up several percent, then your advisor fails to watch it in a down year for the market, you will probably lose money. Was the problem in this hypothetical case the IBM stock? Should you vow to never buy IBM stock again, or any other type of stock? Of course not.

You need to fire the advisor and find someone who knows that s/

he is doing!

Back to the garden example: what is the best vegetable to plant in your garden? Is all corn good and all beans bad? In the same way, a stock, bond, mutual fund, CD or any other type of investment is neither good nor bad. Your profit or loss is much more dependent on how each of these investments is <u>managed</u> rather than on which one(s) you choose.

At some point in time you may have tried to manage your money on your own, using mutual funds that invested in stocks or bonds. You did your best to try to select the right ones, you put your money in, and you left it alone. In some years your funds seemed to do okay, but then a losing year would come along and wipe out several years worth of gains.

You may have even tried investing on your own, using individual stocks or bonds, but you didn't have a systematic process for determining when to buy or when to sell. As a result, you probably got beaten up by the professionals that were on the other side of the trade. There didn't seem to be any rhyme or reason to the markets.

At some point you probably turned to a "professional" advisor because you thought s/he would do a better job. The advisor might have steered your money into mutual funds or a type of annuityand just left it in there regardless of the market's performance.

That's what happened to one of my current clients when he was with a previous advisor. "Bill" retired from his job as an engineer in 2000 and invested his $750,000 nest egg with the local commission-based advisor. The advisor put Bill's money in a variable annuity and even signed him up for an additional service that would time how much was exposed to the market and make changes (there was an additional cost of almost 2% for this "service" that should have been done by the broker in the first place!).

To make a long story short, after three years Bill's $750,000 was worth only $350,000. Like many of you today, Bill was devastated. Instead of enjoying his retirement going fishing and travelling as he had expected, he had to go back to work. That's when he came to me. The problem wasn't that his investments were in the stock market; the problem was that they weren't being managed effectively. Thankfully, Bill is retired once again.

Maybe you are in a situation like Bill. Have you entrusted your retirement savings to an advisor or insurance company only to see it fall in value? Are you at the point of saying enough is enough? There is a better way, a way that will put you back in control and can get you back on track and help you to find the best investments for retirees.

You've tried it on your own and you've tried investing with a traditional advisor. Neither approach worked very well or you wouldn't be reading this report. The problem isn't that you were invested in stocks and bonds, the problem was WHEN you were invested in them. Most investors have been led to believe that the only way to successfully invest is to buy something and let it sit, come hell or high water. They call it Buy and Hold. I call it Buy and Hope. Hope is *not* an investment process.

I can use a tech stock like Ebay to illustrate. If you bought Ebay on September 25th, 1998, you would have paid $1.86 a share. And IF you were lucky enough to have held it and then sold it on March 24, 2000, you would have received $30.47 per share. I'm not a math whiz, but buying something for $1.86 and selling it for $30.47 sounds pretty good to me. That doesn't mean Ebayqualifies as a "good" investment at all times. If you had bought it on October 10th, 2003, you would have paid $30.23 per share. Seven years later it was at $25/share. Thus,"good" depends on when you bought it and when you sold it. Buying low and riding it all the way up doesn't accomplish anything if you wait until it drops all the way back down to sell it.

I've thoroughly discussed the set-it-and-forget-it mind-set and how people use it with pre-packaged investment products such as annuities. The same mind-set can also be applied to how investments like stock and bonds are managed--it doesn't work. If investors have learned anything the past several years,it is that buy and hold *doesn't* work.

The key to getting the income in retirement you need in today's uncertain-interest-rate environment isn't to try to find a new type of investment, but to find those traditional investments that offer the best opportunity based on the current type of market environment, and then to manage them correctly.

Let's assume that you've come to the conclusion that pre-packaged investment products such as annuities aren't the answer. What should you do? What are the best investments for retirees? You have a choice: either invest on your own or get a professional to work with you. Either way, set some ground rules that will help you avoid repeating the mistakes of the past. Here are several that I suggest:

1. I will absolutely retain control over my financial future so that I can make changes or adjustments if and when needed. As a result, I will avoid non-liquid investments and those that require multi-year time commitments or impose large surrender penalties.
2. I will remember that I care more about my money than anyone else, so I recognize I have the ongoing responsibility to monitor my investments. Regardless of whether I manage them myself or with the aid of a professional, I will establish guidelines that determine when I will reduce my exposure to risk assets.
3. I won't take a set-it-and-forget-it mind-set. Therefore I will monitor the value of my investments closely. In volatile markets that may mean weekly. In less volatile markets that may mean monthly or quarterly.
4. I will revisit the "how long will my money last" test to see if I am on track or if I need to make adjustments to my investments and/or my lifestyle.

Do You Need the Help of a Financial Pro? Choosing Between Good, Better and Best

When considering whether you should try to do this yourself or get a professional to work with you, think in terms of good, better and best. And, because you're going to retain control either way, you can always change your mind, something you can't easily do with pre-packaged products.

To restate this: there is much less risk and cost associated with making a choice that doesn't work out this way, compared to the potential loss of tens of thousands of dollars should you want *out* of a pre-packaged product like an annuity.

A "Good" Income Strategy You Can Implement On Your Own

The "good" option is the simplest and doesn't require any special investing knowledge. The risks are easy to see. This option is to rely on ultra-safe investments like CDs (Certificates of Deposit) or government-guaranteed bonds. There are even inflation-protected treasury securities. Frankly, I think you are better off using CDs than buying one of those annuities we've been talking about. They don't fluctuate based on the market and what you see is what you get—there are no hidden surprises. Better yet, you don't risk losing any principal, as you do in an annuity. The most you can lose with a CD is some of the interest you've earned (assuming you are under the $250,000-per-bank limit).

However, you shouldn't put all of your money into a single CD for a couple of reasons. First, you want to spread out when the CD matures because that gives you access without an interest penalty and allows you to reinvest at a higher rate. It's possible that interest rates could be lower a couple of years down the road, but it is more likely that they will be higher. This is referred to as laddering your maturities.

Let's say you have $500,000 that you are going to invest in Certificates of Deposit and all of that money is available right now. Here's an example of a ladder:

Amount	Maturity	Interest Rate
$100,000	1 Year	1.00%
$100,000	2 Years	1.50%
$100,000	3 Years	1.75%
$100,000	4 Years	2.00%
$100,000	5 Years	2.50%

*these rates are hypothetical and do not reflect what is currently available.

Once this ladder was set up, you would have 20% ($100,000) of your money coming due each year. To continue the ladder you would use that money to buy another 5-year CD. If interest rates are generally increasing, you should definitely earn more than you did on the CD that matured because of both higher rates and a longer term. Over time, the average rate becomes equal to the 5-year rate and you still will have money coming due every year.

How long should your ladder be? That depends on how you feel about the direction that interest rates will go. The last thing you want is to be locked in a 5-year CD at 2% and new 5-year CDs paying 5%. Therefore, the more you think rates will go up, the shorter you will want your ladder, so your money comes due and can be reinvested at the higher rate sooner. As rates get higher and higher you can lengthen the time frame, so you can continue to earn the higher rate if other rates decline.

You can ladder CDs so that as rates rise, so will your earnings. You'll still have the flexibility to make changes. There are plenty of ways on the Internet to shop for which banks pay the best rates, and there are even online banks that pay CD-like interest rates on money market accounts. Start slowly.

The second reason you don't want to put all of your money into a single CD is because there are limits to FDIC insurance. If you have more than $250,000 then you definitely will want to use more than one institution, but I would recommend doing so even if you have far less. It's only prudent. In the event a bank goes under, they are typically bought out by another bank and access to your funds isn't affected. There can be situations, though, where you won't have immediate access right away, as people found out in 2008. It's not worth the risk--just use more than one bank.

You don't have to limit yourself to banks in your area, either. You can utilize banks in other states. You can sift through websites to find the most attractive rates on CDs. Just Google "certificate of deposit rates" and there will be a host of options to choose from. Verify that each institution you use is FDIC-insured.

Better

The "better" option includes the types of investments in the "good" option, but not exclusively. Instead, the better option is to spread your money among a variety of investments. The amount and type of investments used will depend on your experience and your comfort level.

If you are ultra-conservative, then you may just want to have the majority of the money in CDs and a smaller portion in a high-quality bond-oriented investment, such as a mutual fund or an exchange-traded fund. The benefit of adding a bond-oriented fund is that it can provide returns higher than those paid by CDs. Of course, the value of the bond fund will fluctuate and you aren't guaranteed of getting back what you put in, but over time I believe that properly managed bond funds can add value.Keep in mind, however, that bond funds do well in some seasons and in others do not. This depends on the type of bond fund, what it invests in and the degree of flexibility that the fund manager has. Typically, bond funds do well in a decreasing-interest-rate-environment and not as well when interest rates are rising. Keep an eye out for "experts" on TV or in popular financial magazines warning that it's time to get out of bonds because interest rates might rise. No one knows what is going to happen to interest rates or the stock market. The "experts" are simply making predictions.

Those same "experts" have been telling us for several years that interest rates were rising and that the "great rotation" (the movement of money in huge amounts from bond-oriented investments to stock-oriented investments) is underway and that we all should sell bonds and buy stocks before it is too late. Unsurprisingly, many of those predicting this rotation will make big money if it happens. In the industry, this is known as "talking your book"—giving advice not just because it is true but because you will be enriched. "Talking your book" is epidemic in this industry, so you should take all market prognostications with a grain of salt.

Do I think that interest rates are going to go up or down? I don't know. So, I do my research and take a stand on what I believe has the highest probability rate in the next 6-12 months. Then, I closely monitor the situation to see if it changes and did or did not work out as expected. I then adjust accordingly.

When it comes to investing, NO ONE will get it right all of the time. The keys are to recognize when you are wrong, minimize the damage and change course.

Let's take a look at a concrete example. Most of the clients I serve are conservative; they want to grow wealth but their top priority is to prevent catastrophic losses. At the start of each year, and several times throughout the year, I try to determine the mix of investments that will give them the best return with the least amount of risk.

To do this, I first identify the general trend of the markets. In 2010, I believed that we were in a longer-term Bear Market cycle even though the market had been recovering. In Bear Market cycles, lower-risk investments such as bonds tend to out-perform higher-risk investments such as stock. Thus, I decided to emphasize conservative investments in 2010. I selected two bond funds and paired them. They rose 20.12% and 8.52% in 2010, respectively.

Meanwhile, the stock market (represented by the Standard and Poor's 500 Index) was up 15.06%, a very attractive return but too high in terms of volatility as the chart below indicates. See if you could stomach the zigzag of the green line:

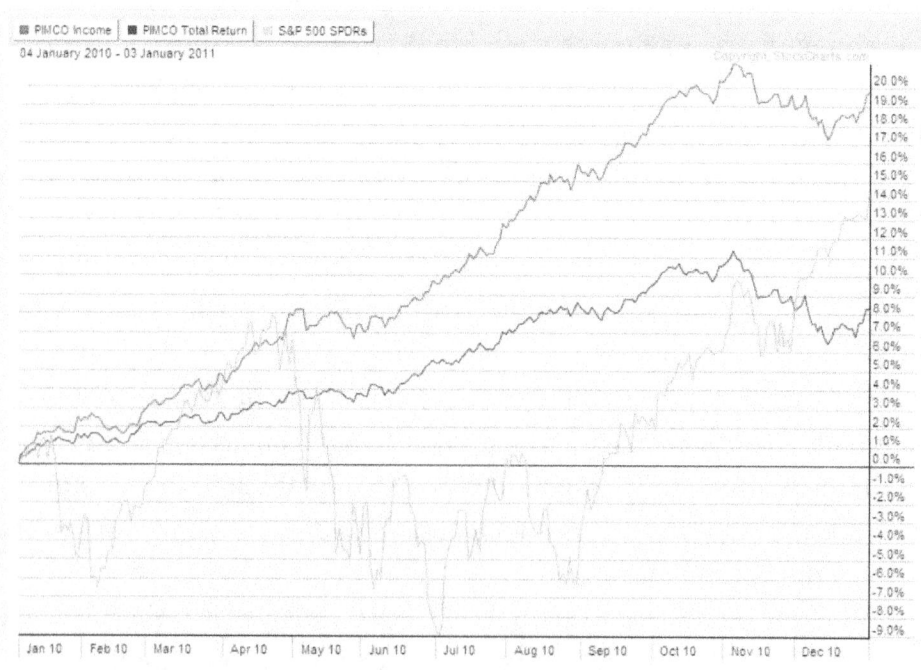

The red and blue lines, which depict the bond funds that I chose, allowed my clients to sleep a lot better than the wild gyrations of the S&P 500 line (green). That line went down between 8% and 17% through the year, while the bond funds never declined more than 6%. Which would you have rather had?

Was 2010 unique? Let's take a look. I held to my thesis for both 2011 and 2012: thatconservative investments such as bonds would provide a greater risk-adjusted return than the general stock market. Take a look at the chart below, which depicts the course that the three options took in 2011:

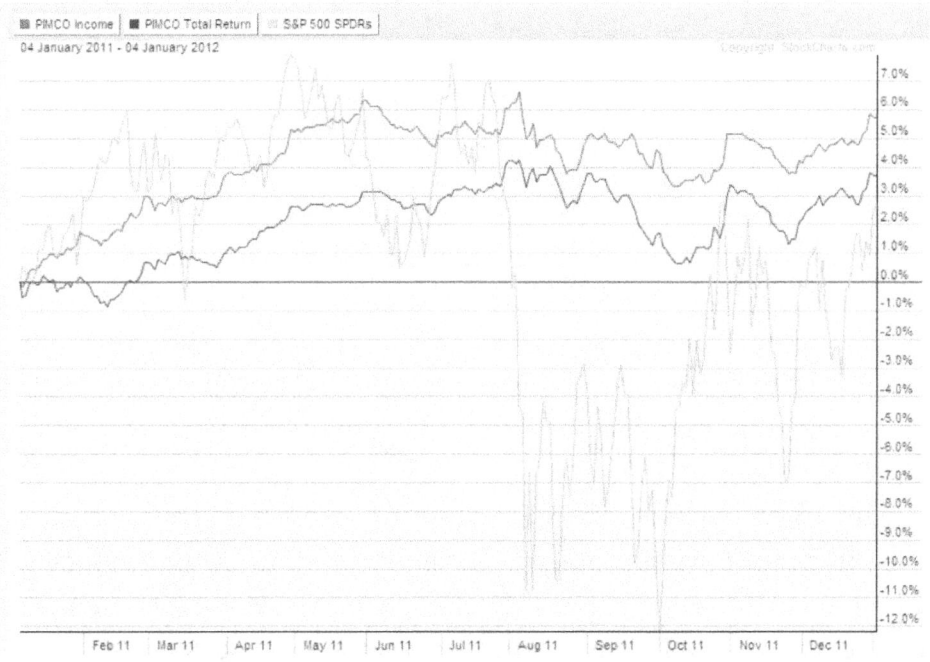

In 2011, the S&P 500 crossed the 0% return line a whopping 18 times! There were several drops of 6+% and a harrowing July/August freefall of almost 18%. After a recovery in August and September, it plunged again, even further, in October.

Meanwhile, the bond funds saw some volatility, but nothing like that of the S&P 500.

Would 2012 follow a similar pattern? I stuck to my guns. Let's see how that worked out:

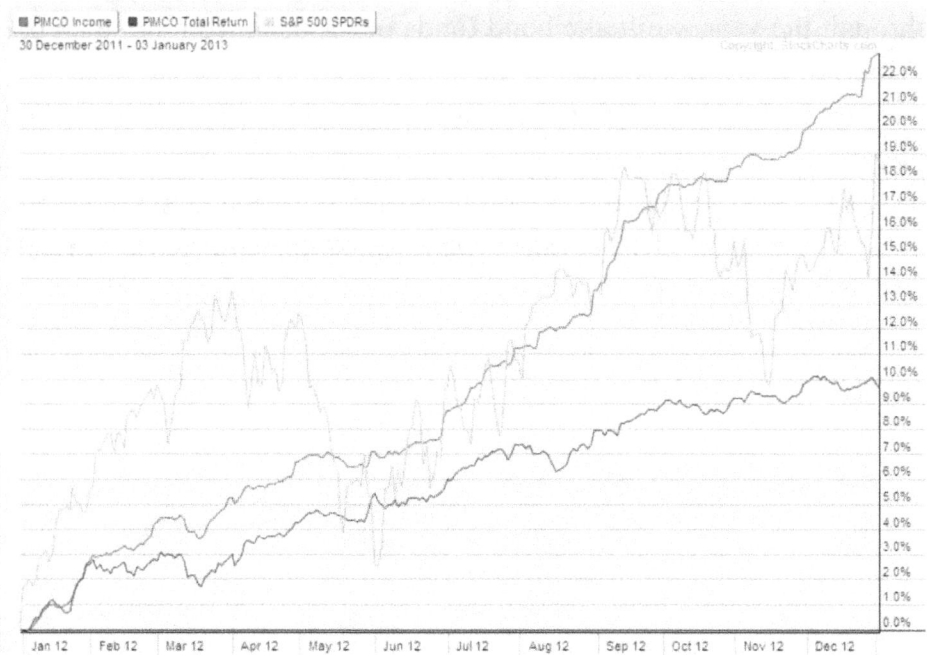

The bond funds rose almost 10% and 22+%, respectively, with a much smoother ride than the S&P 500's line. My clients slept well in 2012 too.

2014 and beyond? There's no way to know, but you *can* get an attractive return without fully exposing yourself to the risk associated with the volatile stock market. Do I believe that retirees should invest in stocks? Absolutely, but it depends on timing and selection.

If we return to Bull Market cycles, then I will increase my client's exposure to stocks because they should provide a better risk-adjusted return than bonds. Remember: how the investments are managed is often more important than the type of investments used.

As you are comfortable with more risk, you can venture into other types of investments such as:

- International or emerging market bond-oriented funds
- Dividend-paying stocks or funds
- High-quality companies that may not pay dividends but have the potential to grow
- Real estate-oriented stocks or funds
- Companies in emerging markets.

The further you go on that list, the more risk you will be taking.

The greater the diversification, the more work involved, and the closer attention you have to pay to your account. You will want to keep an eye on what is going on in the U.S. economy as well as in countries such as China, India, Australia, Canada, Brazil and those in Europe. Because the world is so interconnected, you will also need to understand the impact of changes in the value of the U.S. dollar and interest rates. You don't have to become an expert, but you will need to take the time to read and study if you hope to get in on some of the best investments for retirees.

Keep in mind that you don't have to be fully invested all the time. You can adjust the amount you have in CDs versus bonds and stocks based on your comfort level and what is transpiring in the markets. There are times when it will be better to *not* be in the markets. During those times, try to find higher-interest money market accounts to park the money in while you wait.

The key here is that *you* keep control over your investments and *you* maintain your ability to adjust to changes in your situation or the investing environment. Even once you've invested, keep reading, keep learning and keep researching. It needs to be become a hobby so that you can become more informed over time.

The downside to the "good" and "better" choices is that *you* are the one that has to do the work. You have to closely monitor the values of your accounts. Conditions can change quickly and you will need to take action from time to time. There are also downsides to using mutual funds versus individual stocks. These options are both better than the pre-packaged products discussed in this report, but they still aren't the best way.

Find a Process That Works For You

As with many processes in life, investing successfully takes a lot of time and hard work; there aren't any shortcuts or secret investments out there that no one else knows about. You aren't going to be able to look at a few websites and be able to come to a decision. It is going to take time and it's going to take effort—if you want to do it right.

For example, my wife and I recently needed to buy a new dishwasher. In view of the many brands and options to choose from, we did research on the Internet before going to the store. We looked at reviews and researched features, and this made the decision of which one to buy much easier.

You probably take time to do research when you make a major purchase, too. Nowadays, the Internet makes it so easy to find information and opinions that many of us do research even before we make smaller purchases.

You need to approach your search for the best investments for retirees in the same way. There are many aspects that you can research, but instead of jumping right in to look at specific companies, I suggest you first research an investment <u>process</u>, a pre-defined method for determining when to buy and when to sell.

You can manage traditional investments in many ways to help <u>reduce</u> the risk of loss and <u>increase</u> the probability of making money. You have to find and develop a process that works for you. That *doesn't* mean the process has to involve a complex mathematical algorithm. You don't have to hire programmers and spend tens of thousands of dollars as private, personal money managers likeI have. The key is that your process should fit who you are and be repeatable.

Keep in mind that when you are starting out, every process will sound like a winner. You will need to dig deeper to understand how they work, and then you should go back and test each strategy during various market time periods. If you are considering using an investment newsletter to find stocks to buy and when to buy and sell them, don't rely on what the newsletter tells you their return is—get back issues of the newsletter (several years if possible) and start at the first one and begin verify that what they say is true. Don't just track the rate of return, track both the return and the amount of volatility someone had to endure to get that return. See if the newsletter recommended hanging on to stocks during the crash in 2008. Research it like you would any other important purchase; research is required whatever route you take.

For instance, let's say the process you are considering involves buying when the stock is above its 50-day moving average and selling when it drops below it. You can use historical prices found at Yahoo Finance (http://finance.yahoo.com/) and play "what if." Pick a few starting dates and then track how you would have done using this method. This won't guarantee that you will choose the best method, but it will help you better understand how it works in different markets.

The type of method that works best is going to vary based on market conditions. That's why wise private money managers diversify their clients' portfolios by *method* as well as investments. Then, they closely monitor the methods to see how they are working. If the methods being used don't work as expected, they see it as their responsibility to try to find one that does.

Thus, even after you find a method that you want to use, your process may change over time. You should also consider trading with your method as a test with a small amount of money. I like this better than "paper trading," because when you are emotionally involved, the decisions can be different, and using real money will make you emotionally involved.

For beginner investors, know that you can dramatically increase your potential for gains and minimize your losses just by basing when to buy and sell on the relationship of a stock to its moving average.

For instance, let's say you want to decide whether it's time to invest in the U.S. Stock Market. You can pull up a chart of the S&P 500 and superimpose a 200-day moving average (200 DMA) on it. (http://www.google.com/finance?q=INDEXSP:.INX) Click on the word "Technicals" at the bottom left of the chart, choose "simple moving average SMA" from the dropdown and enter 200 in the period box. Then click "Add Technical." In the upper left of the chart window where it says "zoom," click on the word "All" and the chart will then show the index from 1971 to 2010.

As you can see, the S&P 500 (blue line) was higher than its 200

DMA most of the time between 1980 and 2010. If all that you did was buy the S&P 500 (SPY) when the index was above its 200 DMA and sold it when it dropped below, you would have profited from the major upward movements while avoiding the worst declines.

Let's see how you would have fared from 2000 to 2010. We'll assume that the investor waited until the first time the index was below the 200 DMA and then crossed back above it. I'm using weekly data supplied by Google.

Date	Action	Price	% Gain
April 20th, 2001	Buy	1242.98	
June 15th, 2001	Sell	1214.36	-2%
January 16th, 2004	Buy	1139.83	
March 19th, 2004	Sell	1109.78	-3%
April 2nd, 2004	Buy	1141.81	
May 7th, 2004	Sell	1098.70	-4%
May 28th, 2004	Buy	1120.68	
August 6th, 2004	Sell	1063.97	-5%
August 20th, 2004	Buy	1098.35	
March 7th, 2008	Sell	1293.37	18%
March 20th, 2008	Buy	1329.51	
June 20th, 2008	Sell	1317.93	-1%

Total Gain Over 10 Years: 3%

Buy & Hold

Date	Action	Price	% Gain
October 1st, 2000	Buy	1436.51	
September 30th, 2010	Sell	1146.24	-20%

200 DMA Process Vs. Buy and Hold: +17%

A couple of lessons can be learned from this result. First, using this process (+3%) produced much better results than Buy and Hold (-20%). Earning 3% from 2000-2010 isn't anything to get excited about--unless you bought and held and lost 20%!

Second, the investor using this process still would have had significant draw-downs (declines from a peak to a trough) and may not have been able to stick with the process.

The 200 DMA is just an example. You can modify it by using a shorter duration. For instance, you can try a 100 DMA or a 50 DMA.

The lower number of days chosen will result in a higher number of trades, but will also enable you to get out of the market quicker when it starts to go down and in faster when it starts to go up.

There are other data points that you can incorporate when you develop your process. You might want to take a look at the fundamentals of a company. Fundamentals help you see whether or not the company is making a profit, gives you a general idea of how it is being valued by the market relative to other similar companies. In my mind, fundamental factors impact the long-term trend of the company but don't always indicate the best time to buy or sell. Technical indicators such as moving averages, chart lines, stochastics, relative strength indicators, etc., are designed to help identify entry and exit points. Some managers seem to rely solely on fundamental factors, whereas others may rely solely on technical ones. Perhaps incorporating parts of both may be beneficial—it all depends on your style and interests.

The goal is to develop a systematic process that can help you determine what to buy, when to buy it and when to sell it. If you choose to go this route, it needs to be something that you enjoy and are willing to invest many hours in. You will need to thoroughly test many systems while keeping in mind that you are "battling" against some of the sharpest minds on Wall Street.

On the other hand, you don't have to out-perform the best minds, just other individual investors! Even after you settle on a system, continue to monitor it closely and don't be afraid to pull the plug if it stops working. It's crucial to determine the type of market a given system performs best in and then only use it in that market.

If you are an investing novice and unsure of yourself, you can start with the "good" option. You can then take the time to familiarize yourself more with the markets and eventually graduate to the "better" option. I have to be honest, though. If you haven't invested before, or if you are an experienced investor that doesn't want to spend hours a day doing research and making decisions, then you are better off finding a qualified professional to work with you.

Best

The "best" option is not something you can do on your own. You will need the help of a private money manager, someone that actually manages money dayin and dayout. This gives you the best of both worlds. You can retain control and oversight, but hire someone to handle the day-to-day implementation. That way you don't have to be involved daytoday or week to week, but neither are you divorcing yourself from what is going on.

You have a choice of professionals to work with, and there are many out there, but few are what I am referring to as new-era "private money managers."

There are a lot of different terms used in the financial services industry and, as aninvestor, it is easy to become confused. Two people can use the same title and yet have vastly different duties. That's why I've tried to use terms like "traditional advisor," "money management firm" and "personal money manager" to describe different approaches and to allow you to distinguish between the services they offer.

A "traditional advisor" refers to a person that works at firms like EdwardJones, Merrill Lynch, AG Edwards or Morgan Stanley. These advisors go by titles such as "Investment Representative," "Broker," "In vestment Advisor," "Registered Representative," etc. They traditionally sell investments based on commission, but over the past few years have begun offering fee-based alternatives.

I also include insurance agents in this category because, even though they are not licensed to give investment advice (nor do they have <u>any</u> background or training to do so), that distinction is often lost on the person seeking their help. *All* insurance agents work on commission. They say that they get paid by the insurance company, but do you really believe that it's not going to come out of your pocket?

Some "independent" advisors aren't associated with the big firms mentioned above. These advisors typically contract with another firm to provide back-office services; some are fee-based, others are commission-based and some are both. Many independent advisors are "registered investment advisors" (RIAs). One thing that differentiates RIAs from commissioned advisors is that RIAs have a fiduciary responsibility to act in their client's best interest, whereas commission-based advisors and insurance agents do not. That means that RIAs are held to a much higher legal standard to do what is in your best interest.

You can't tell how someone is regulated or whether they have training and experience based on what they call themselves. As a result, you can be talking to an insurance agent thinking that s/he has the licenses needed to offer any investment, when s/he might only offer insurance products.

The term "money management firm" refers to companies whose primary focus is money management. They don't do financial plans, don't sell insurance products, etc. Money management firms handle the day-to-day selection of stocks or bonds and decide when to buy and sell them. In many respects, the services provided by a money management firm are similar to those provided by a mutual fund and hedge funds.

Since what I and others like me do doesn't fit in any of the above categories; I use the term "privatemoney manager" to try to avoid confusion. For instance, I do not hold a securities license, so I can't sell investments on commission. I am organized as a Registered Investment Advisor and function under the oversight of the Securities and Exchange Commission (SEC) or the Securities Division associated with the states in which I do business. I do have an insurance license, which means I can sell products such as life insurance, immediate annuities, fixed indexed annuities and long-term care on commission.

I also provide general financial planning services, so in many respects I function like many financial planning fee-based advisors. I also provide the day-to-day money management provided by a money management firm.

The Pros and Cons of Working with a New-Era Private Money Manager

Advantages and Disadvantages

There are advantages and disadvantages to working with a privatemoney manager compared to a money management firm or a traditional advisor:

Advantage #1: You have a personal relationship with the person managing your money.

One of the main problems in working with a traditional advisor, a money management firm, a mutual fund or an insurance company is that there is a disconnect between the investor and the person making the day-to-day decisions of what is in the portfolio. With any of these options, there is always a middleperson between you and the one managing your money.

The gap between you and the one managing your money will vary depending on the category of advisor you choose. It is very wide when working with a traditional advisor, because the person making the day-to-day decisions affecting your portfolio probably doesn't even work for the same company as the advisor, nor is there communication between the advisor and the money manager regarding your situation.

In this case, the goals of each participant are different, and they often are not aligned with *your* goals. The advisor is focused on getting as many clients as s/he can because that is how s/he makes money. The money manager is focused on keeping the boss happy so s/he can be moved to a bigger pool of money.

You might already realize this because you have experienced it. While you were led to believe that your account would receive a lot of personal attention, you soon realized that wasn't the case. This became even more apparent when the markets were volatile and little, if any, action was taken.

This gap also exists when you work with a money management firm, because these firms are designed to work with a large number of investors and manage as much money as they can. That's why they have people that function as account managers, because it is impractical for the money manager to interface with a large number of clients. Your contact is with the account manager, so once again a middleperson is involved and a disconnect results between you and the one making the day-to-day decisions affecting your portfolio.

I believe this disconnect is the main reason for investor dissatisfaction. You *know* your money is not being closely monitored. You are being treated like everyone else, but your needs don't match everyone else's.

Clients who have a private money manager have a close relationship with the person making the day-to-day decisions affecting the value of their portfolio, sans the typical disconnect caused by a middleperson. From the very beginning of the relationship, the client interacts with the manager, and when s/he has questions about the account s/he talks directly with the manager.

If the manager needs more information about how you want to

proceed and what actions you want taken, s/he works <u>directly</u> with you. Suchinteractionallows the relationship between you and the manager to deepen over time. The deeper the relationship, the better the manager will be able to act according to your needs and desires. S/he will understand what makes you uncomfortable and adjust how your portfolio is managed when your situation or comfort level changes.

Advantage #2: You can directly influence the strategies and methods that are used.

Because a traditional advisor hands off the money management to an outside group, you are limited to the managers his/her firm uses. In the end, it's really no different than using a mutual fund. Several groups can be chosen, each with a different focus and philosophy, but you won't have any input into how they manage your money. Even if separate account management is used, your money is still lumped in with everyone else's and managed the same way.

Money management firms also focus on a single money management philosophy and have pre-defined buckets that you select from. For instance, the firm may follow a buy-and-hold philosophy and only use large, well-established companies. That means that its approach won't change as the market does; it will stick to the same philosophy regardless of market and economic conditions. In operation, again, it's really not that different than investing in a mutual fund.

That's not how it works for clients that have a private money manager. You have a much greater influence on the philosophy, strategy and even the individual investments used in your account. You receive a level of customization that doesn't exist anywhere else, because there is no way a firm can deliver the level of service that a private money manager does.

You also aren't limited by the "single philosophy" approach used by most money managers. I've advised investors through up-and-down markets, and one lesson I've learned the hard way is that each broad philosophy has a certain type of market that it does best in. There isn't a single philosophy that does equally as well in all market environments. That's why a good private money manager will shift the applied philosophy based on the type of market in play.

Another feature that separates a private money manager from everyone else is the diversification by philosophy s/he employs. If it makes sense to spread your "eggs" among cash, stocks, bonds and real estate to reduce risk, doesn't it also make sense that your account be diversified by the overriding philosophy that is used? The concept of diversification is based on the idea that there will be times when a stock does well and times when a bond performs better. By using multiple, negativelycorrelated (moving in opposite directions) investments and managing them with diversity of philosophy, the overall risk can be reduced even further.

Another advantage when you work with a private money manager is that you have access to a variety of strategies and processes and can even recommend additional ones. A strategy is different from a philosophy. If, for example, the value of the U.S. dollar drops precipitously, as it has a few times in recent years, the prices of commodities like corn, oil and copper tend to rise. Therefore, one strategy that could be used is to invest in those commodities, in the companies that benefit from higher commodity prices or in countries that are rich in natural resources.

You don't have any input into those types of decisions when you work with traditional advisors or money management firms, but you can with a private money manager. Some clients want to be involved in that level of discussion and others don't—it's up to them.

You also get a level of customization that isn't available elsewhere. Your portfolio can be totally unique and customized. For instance, I have several clients that are retired from ExxonMobil who had large holdings of the company stock. We were able to customize their portfolio to account for that.

Perhaps there are certain types of investments you don't want used in your account, e.g., stocks in master limited partnerships. That's easily taken care of. You can even tell a private money manager that you don't want to buy a specific company like Nike for whatever reason. That's no problem; it won't be in your account even though it may be a stock that is a part of a strategy being used in your account.

You can imagine the difficulty in providing this level of service and customization, and you might even think it's impossible to do. In a sense, you're right. It's not humanly possible unless a private money manager only has a few clients. How can s/he possibly do this for 100 clients?

The Portfolio Steward

To solve this problem, I have spent years developing proprietary software, strategies, processes and systems. I've done so because I recognized that I needed tremendous flexibility to be able to manage each client's money as if s/he were my only account. I understand that each client is unique and so are his/her needs.

There is software available for all sorts of money management goals. Some software helps money management firms to manage a pool of money, other software allows money managers to use algorithmic trading, and still other software helps advisors to track a client's portfolio and apply standard allocations across multiple accounts.

However, there wasn't any software designed for an advisor who was also a money manager. No software existed that combined the ability to make a large number of trades using multiple trading systems with the client portfolio management needs of an advisor.

So, I created my own.

The software gives the flexibility to customize what is used in each client's account while automating a lot of the background tasks. It allows me to create pre-defined conditions under which something should be bought or sold. Multiple trading systems can be created by mixing and matching the buy and sell components. Each security can be associated with multiple trading systems.

The beauty of the system is that once it is set up and the allocations are assigned to an account, the system recognizes what is currently owned and whether there is cash available. If there is cash available to invest, it uses the allocations to create a target buy list specifically for that account. The system then monitors securities on that customized buy list and alerts me when the pre-defined conditions have been met. The purchase can be made with a few clicks of a mouse!

In all of this finely calculated system I use multiple currencies to trade on various markets around the world, depending on the risk that I am trying to avoid. That made the creation of this software more complicated for me, but it keeps your choices fairly simple. This flexibility is another valuable component of my investing philosophy. Globalization is here to stay, and you should not miss out on any hot stocks that are skyrocketing on other continents.

My ability to serve as both an advisor and money manager, while providing the ability to tailor what happens to the individual needs of each client, is only possible through this software, which I call The Portfolio Steward. I have been awarded three U.S. patents on it; it allows me to assist each client in a way that would otherwise be humanly impossible. Other private money managers don't have access to the Portfolio Steward, but they might have their own processes and procedures. When selecting a private money manager, be sure to find out what his/her internal processes are so that you can understand how your money will be managed.

Even though a private money manager's day-to-day priority is managing the client's money, s/he should still be available to help the client with general financial planning. In the same way that you need to understand a private money manager's investment processes, you should also find out about their financial planning philosophy. The reason is that the manager's processes will be built on an underlying philosophy, and you need to dig a little deeper and discover what the manager's philosophy is. Does it center on the old wisdom that the past can predict the future? Does it call for quick adjustments to the processes when the market conditions change? Many of you reading this report have lost money because the philosophy of your advisor was outdated and inflexible. Find out about a private money manager's philosophy before you entrust your money to him/her.

A philosophy that relies too heavily on past performance is now outdated, and I would use Bill Miller of Legg Mason Capital Management as a perfect example. Miller has been the portfolio manager for the Legg Mason Value Trust since its inception in 1982. Years ago it was considered one of the best mutual funds *ever* and Miller received numerous awards. According to Wikipedia:

> "SmartMoney ranked Miller among the top 30 most influential people in investing.[3] Money magazine named Miller as 'The Greatest Money Manager of the 1990's.' Morningstar named him 'Domestic Equity Manager of the Year' in 1998 and 'Fund Manager of the Decade' in 1999.[4] In 1999, Miller was named to Barron's Mutual Funds 'All-Century Team.' *BusinessWeek* called him one of the 'Heroes of Value Investing' in 1999."[2]

Miller was a value investor in the tradition of Ben Graham and it served him well--until value investing stopped working. It had a negative return in 2007, underperforming the S&P 500 by 11%. In 2008, the Legg Mason Value Trust was down 55%. Few investors would have expected that kind of a loss from a manager with such a stellar past performance record.

Past performance can also be skewed by a great return in a single year. If a manager has a good 2010, it will reflect not just in their 2010 performance but also in their 1-, 3-, 5- and 10-year performance. The Legg Mason Value Trust had an amazing run and excellent long-term performance until 2005. Now, it lags the S&P 500 for 3-, 5- and 10-

---

2 http://en.wikipedia.org/wiki/Bill_Miller_(finance), retrieved 6/9/13

year periods and receives just one star from Morningstar ratings.[3]

My approach to financial planning is a very practical one. It is often the weakest link in your overall financial "chain" that exposes you to the potential for significant financial loss, thus I focus on discovering and repairing those weak links.

For instance, there is a medical doctor that I'll call Sam. Sam and his wife were about 50 years old and had a thriving medical practice, but they were too busy to give their personal finances the attention they needed. When they first came to see me, Sam was concerned about his wife being taken care of were he to die. We updated their estate plan and reviewed their insurance coverage. I helped them refinance their home so that they saved $25,000 in interest each year.

Now Sam and his wife can sleep at night knowing that even if his cancer returns and he passes away, she will be taken care of. They are incredibly relieved to have found someone that they can trust.

Then there is Rick and Mary Ann. They desperately wanted to retire but were afraid that they didn't have enough money. We met and I was able to show them how they could retire whenever they wanted, thanks to a few adjustments.

When you work with a private manager you will have a trusted advisor that you can turn to for advice on every area of your financial life.Others might charge hundreds or thousands of dollars for that kind of advice, but that counsel is typically included in the private money manager's money management fee at no extra charge.

Advantage #3: It's cheaper than working with a traditional advisor.

Assuming the same underlying investment performance, every 1% you save in advisor/money management fees is an extra 1% you earn. Earning an extra 1% doesn't seem as important when there are annual returns greater than 10%, but in today's environment where 5-7%

---

3 http://www.google.com/finance?q=MUTF:LMVTX&sa=X&ei=rO 21UYTwBqm80gHV54GQDw&ved=0CEIQ2AE, retrieved 6/6/13

may be typical, saving 1% is a big deal. Compared to working with a traditional advisor using a variable annuity, clients of a private money manager save a lot more than 1%. That makes achieving their goals much easier.

The bottom line is always going to be performance, and you don't want to be penny wise and pound foolish. There aren't any fees associated with a CD, but that doesn't mean that it offers the best after-fee return potential, so you can't focus solely on fees. Lower fees will impact performance, but the processes and systems used to determine when to buy and sell those investments has a much greater impact.

Take 2008 as an example. There were low-cost stock market investments available from companies like Vanguard. The fees on some of their funds were only 10 basis points (that's $1/10^{th}$ of 1%) whereas the typical private money manager's fee is 1% to 1.25%, depending on the amount managed. Those owning the Vanguard fund saved a lot in fees compared to a private money manager's client, but they lost far more due to market losses. The actions that a good private money manager should have taken that year would have saved his/her clients many years' worth of management fees. Fees are important, but proper management even more so.

In some cases, a private money manager's fees are lower than those charged by other money managers. Hedge funds charge a 2% management fee and then take 20% of any profits. It's not uncommon for non-hedge fund money managers to charge 1.5% or more. Those using sophisticated processes can charge 2% or more.

The fees in a variable annuity with a guaranteed income stream and automatic annual increases can quickly surpass 4% a year. That's another reason why I feel they aren't a good investment. The "guarantees" and "riders" are used to distract the investor from the true underlying performance of the subaccounts, and that true performance will be severely impacted by those ongoing annual fees. Imagine having to earn 4% a year in these markets just to break even! Money markets in variable annuities can actually have negative returns as a result of the fees.

Even though a private money manager provides a level of service and sophisticated money management systems that you can't find anywhere else, s/he doesn't charge as much as most of the alternatives. The end result is a better overall value for you.

Now, you can certainly find ways in which allowing a private money manager to manage your money is inferior to simply putting it into a mutual fund. For instance, a private money manager cannot possibly churn out standardized performance numbers like a mutual fund can. His/her system cannot be boiled down to a standardized return percentage, as a mutual fund's can. The Securities and Exchange Commission (SEC) imposes regulations on privatemoney managers about the disclosure of performance numbers that are so strict, it practically prevents them from doing so. Get references in lieu of performance numbers if you can.

While on the subject of performance numbers, let me say that very few investors ever earn the returns advertised by a mutual fund or money manager because they can be based on a model, not actual accounts. Your return in a mutual fund depends on the exact days that you enter and exit the fund, making your return entirely dependent on your timing. That could be very different from what you have seen advertised for that fund.

The mutual fund market research firm Dalbar found, for instance, that the average annual return for a U.S. stock mutual fund was 11.6% between 1988 and 2007, while the average stock fund investor's return was just 4.5% because it was based on actual cash inflows and outflows. It's all about the timing; beware of performance numbers.[4]

Let's address a few of the perceived disadvantages of investing through a new-era private money manager:

---

4 For details on this discrepancy, see http://www.truenorth-fn.com/newsletters/2008%20Aug%20Mutual%20Fund%20Returns.pdf.

Disadvantage #1: No Standardized Performance Reporting

When selecting mutual funds or money management firms, people typically focus on performance even though "past performance is no guarantee of future performance." I use performance as a means to compare mutual funds in the event I need to use one. Many people think that the best way to judge a private money manager is by his/her performance. There are big differences, though, between the performance reporting done by mutual funds and that by money management firms.

There is a difference in the way the accounts are handled when you use a money manager versus a mutual fund as well. When you use a money manager, your money is not put into a large pool as it is with a mutual fund, but it is managed in each client's account separately. In a mutual fund, you don't see the internal trades that take place. If the mutual fund sells IBM today and buys Cisco, those orders do not show in your account. They do show in your account when you work with a money manager.

The performance reported by mutual funds is based on the daily closing share price. This is an exact representation of the value a shareholder would pay if s/he bought shares that day. It's the exact value s/he would receive per share on the day they were sold. Thus, if you purchased that fund on the first day of the time period, held and then sold the shares on the last day of the reporting period, you would have the same return as those shown in the performance reports.

It doesn't work that way with a private money manager. The performance you would have received could be considerably different from what was reported for several reasons. First, if you put your money in a mutual fund today, it is "fully invested" in that fund. If you invest your money with a money manager today, it probably will not be "invested" today—if the manager is acting in your best interest. Your return is based on the actual price received when the underlying investments are bought or sold in your account. It's not based on the end-of-day value of the overall "pool" being managed.

For instance, let's assume that I have 10 stocks in a strategy that I'm using in other accounts and (after discussing it) we decide we want to use that strategy in your account. All 10 of those stocks may have been purchased over the past few months in other clients' accounts when their prices were much lower. If your money arrives in the account I will be managing for you today, it will not be fully invested right away because now may not be a good time to buy each of them. It is not in your best interest for me to buy every stock in a strategy just because the money hit the account that day.

IBM may have been a great buy at $100 per share when I bought it for other accounts, but it may not be a good time to buy today if it's at $150 per share. Thus the "performance" of your account is going to be different than the performance of the other accounts I manage, even though the same strategy may be used.

Can you see how it is to your benefit that I don't buy everything just because the money hit your account today? Unfortunately, that's not how most money managers do it, because it takes a lot more work on the money manager's end. It's simpler for them to just click a button and buy all the stocks so your account mirrors everyone else's…except your performance won't ever be the same unless you just happened to have received the exact same price today as when it was bought for everyone else previously.

The only way that I have the ability to "individually" manage each account is because of the software that I've developed. Other "separately managed account" managers still work with a mutual fund-type mentality. They are not managing your account individually. I do. The buy and sell decisions that occur in your account are based on what occurs in your account; with other money managers, all the accounts are "in sync." All of my client's accounts are not "in sync" because they are truly managed individually. It makes it harder for a prospective client to gauge my performance this way, but it's to my clients' benefit.

When a money manager reports performance, they are not reporting the performance of actual accounts but of a "model" account. The performance of the model account may not be indicative of the actual performance received in any account. A model account is a paper-based, simulated account where the trades done for that "portfolio" are recorded. The model account may not be in sync with any actual account, so there could be a trade in the model account when there aren't any trades at that time in actual accounts.

Performance reporting is one area that the SEC closely monitors because it can unduly influence an investor to use a manager. As a result, there is a lot of incentive for the manager to boost their performance to the maximum, but SEC rules strictly regulate how performance can be reported so that managers do not "cherry pick." The easiest way for a manager to comply with these restrictions is to use the "model" account approach.

So, even though performance needs to be taken into account when comparing money managers, you have to realize the limitations inherent in it. Just because a manager's performance looks spectacular on paper doesn't mean you will experience it.

I also want to add a word on your personal relationship with your money manager and the guilt that you might feel if you break your relationship with him or her. You might have a wonderful relationship with your manager and be the closest of friends, but be honest: it's all about the decisions that your manager makes and how they affect the value of your account. You work with an advisor/money manager because of what s/he can do for your account, not how friendly s/he is. All too often, people allow their personal relationship with an advisor to affect their business relationship with him/her. Don't make that mistake.

Disadvantage #2: Continuity

Another perceived disadvantage of working with a private money manager like me is the concern over what would happen to the account in the event I were killed or disabled. That's a valid concern and something I would want to know if I were you. In reality, though, it's no different than working with a traditional advisor in that if something were to happen to me. In the event of my death, my practice would be sold. You would have the choice to stay with the new advisor brought in, start managing the account yourself or transfer to another advisor.

There is one advantage in working with me that is related to continuity. I own my own firm, and there's little chance of me leaving the industry or transferring to another firm. Nowadays, it seems like traditional advisors are leaving all the time. They are either getting fired and someone else is assigned to your account or they move to another firm. My clients find that there is a stability associated with my situation that they don't find elsewhere.

Disadvantage #3: Location

Another perceived disadvantage is that a private money manager might be located in a different time zone from you. There are so few of us that it is very unlikely that there is one in your city—even if you live in a large one. When you think about it, though, when have you sat down face-to-face with the person that was managing your money? If your advisor used mutual funds or annuities, you've never met the person handling the day-to-day decisions affecting the value of your account. With the Internet, it's easy to have a face-to-face conversation with anyone around the world. Don't let location keep you from getting the best investment management you can find.

Retain Full Control of Your Money AND Get the Guidance You Need

Remember that you will *always* care more about your money than anyone else, so you need to choose your advisor and investment plan wisely. You can't "setitandforgetit" and hope to make a livable retirement income. You don't necessarily have to monitor your account every day, but you do need to keep tabs on what the money manager is doing.

Because you can see every trade in your account, you will be able to see periods when there is more activity and when there is less. Ask yourself, "Based on what is going on in the economy and the markets, does this activity make sense to me?" If it doesn't, then you should ask questions about why your advisor is doing what s/he is doing.

Many managers seem to follow the same playbook. Does your manager do the same as everyone else or is s/he taking a different path? Frankly, you don't need a manager that thinks the same way everyone else does because you can accomplish the same result on your own with an index fund!

As a money manager, the hardest thing to do is often the best thing to do. Everyone talks about buying low and selling high, but few have the guts to actually do it, and studies have shown that individual investors have a habit of doing just the opposite! Even though the S&P 500 has gone up substantially in the past few weeks or months, it doesn't mean that it is a "safe" time to invest. Recall the charts shown earlier in this report that compared the return of select bond funds with the S&P 500 in 2010, 2011 and 2012. The S&P did well, but the annual return numbers didn't accurately reflect the incredible volatility that had to be endured to achieve that return. Don't forget that in today's global markets, a single piece of news anywhere in the world can cause the markets to change course. This is why having robust risk management processes in place is vital.

Risk is inherent whether the market is bullish or bearish. The nature of a Bear Market rally (an up-trend in a generally down-trending market) is that it is actually stronger than Bull Market rallies. I think of the market in early 2013, for example. Everyone was piling into the same stocks. Hedge funds had not performed well and those fund managers were under tremendous pressure to get returns, so they were chasing the same stocks. At some point there was going to be a rush for the exits and the markets were going to see a very sharp correction, which is precisely what occurred in May and June. We saw the market drop 5-7% just several weeks after this rush to the same stocks.

A great example of the persistent inconsistency of the market today is Apple stock. It was the darling of mutual fund and hedge fund managers through 2012. At one point, more than 240 managers had significant holdings of AAPL, and its price surged. Investors were lured by this increase, even after it had risen 50%. However, it crashed even more quickly than it skyrocketed, because once it started declining, those 250 performance-chasing managers (many of whom had purchased stock with borrowed money) were forced to sell to cover margin calls. Individual and even many professional investors took a bath (see below):

These days, everyone is suddenly becoming bullish. They're jumping back into the market because the Federal Reserve has signaled that it may do further quantitative easing, but historically, quantitative easing hasn't ever worked (see: Japan). Interest rates are still super-low, our country's deficits continue to soar Yet, even after all of this stimulus our economy fails to gain traction. Wall Street may be surging ahead but Main Street is still struggling to survive.

Consequently, my clients' current exposure to equities is very small. Generally speaking, for most of this year I have had a large portion of each account allocated to bonds. Bonds have provided very healthy returns with a small fraction of the volatility associated with stocks. There's simply no reason to unnecessarily expose my clients. I do have a small percentage of the accounts allocated to equities, but that has mostly been moved to cash. In early 2013 I began to allocate more money into U.S. equities, utilizing strategies to quickly exit in the event the market turned down.

The reason that I went into such detail about what I am doing with my clients' accounts is so you can get a feel for the way that a private money manager might approach the markets and the attitude s/he might take with the money they manage on your behalf. Each private money manager is different. Some will be more aggressive than others. Some might react quickly to changes in the markets while others will react slowly. Whether you use my services or those of another manager, you need to feel comfortable with your manager's actions and reasoning. You need to take the time to get to know your prospective private money manager and understand his/her philosophy and temperament. You also need to understand who they are and what drives them personally, because that will impact their investment decisions and approach. Character matters, as do values. Do you share the same values as your prospective manager? Then your relationship will go much better.

Finally, you need to be clear on how your prospective manager will communicate with you and how often s/he will do that. I try to keep my clients updated on what I am doing and why through regular briefings, conference calls, emails and personal conversations.

You will want to be more involved and watch the value of your accounts more closely during the early stages of working with a new private moneymanager. The manager needs to earn your trust through his/her actions. You probably have experienced advisors that did nothing while your account lost money—do the actions of the current manager indicate that s/he will be different? If not, you probably have the wrong manager. Over time, once trust is established, you don't have to check the accounts as often, but you still need to stay engaged.

Keep in mind that each money manager has a system. Unless you have enough money to be his/her only client, then you will have to fit into the system. That means that you have to find the system that comes closest to what you would do if you were handling the investments yourself. Find out what your prospective manager bases his/her buy and sell decisions on, what determines the amount allocated to different types of investments and the overall philosophy s/he has about how markets work. If you are an experienced investor, you need to ask yourself what the manager does that you can't do yourself—and it if is worth what s/he charges to free up your time!

You know what your comfort level is better than anyone. So think about past market declines when you lost money. What would you have liked an advisor to do? Find out what actions were taken by the private moneymanager you are considering and see if s/he would have achieved a better result *and* if you would have been able to sleep at night in the midst of it. You want to focus on the actions taken by the manager to see how they line up with your pain tolerance.

A manager may have taken actions that resulted in a tremendous gain but put the portfolio at increased risk in doing so. Just because the result was a gain doesn't mean it was suitable for your portfolio.

I would also avoid "one-trick-pony" money managers who have a single investment approach. For instance, some money managers only do value investing, others just for growth. Some may just do trading and nothing longterm. The problem is that there isn't a single method that is going to work all the time. That's why I use multiple approaches in the typical account. More importantly, if the approach I'm taking doesn't seem to be working, then I try to find something that is. Not all private money managers do that, but I think it is critical.

Ways To Make Sure Your Money Is Safe

We've all heard of Bernie Madoff and how unsuspecting investors lost billions of dollars because of fraud. There are steps that you can take to make sure something similar doesn't happen to you. You need to:

1) Make sure the manager does NOT have access to your money.

Your account shouldn't be with the money manager. Instead, the account should be at a well-recognized, established national custodian such as Fidelity, Charles Schwab, TDAmeritrade or RaymondJames, etc. The account should be in your name, not the name of the advisor, and you should have access to account statements directly from the custodian. You can then compare the statements from the custodian to the information provided by the advisor to verify that they reconcile.

There are some advisors that take custody of your assets. Don't allow that! You open yourself up to a much greater level of risk. One exception to that rule is a hedge fund. It's normal for a hedge fund to have custody because your money is pooled with that of everyone else's. Most people reading this report won't ever work with a hedge fund because it entails a much greater level of risk than the typical investor will tolerate.

The manager should not be able to transfer money between your accounts. If s/he can, it's a sign that s/he has access to your funds and can transfer it to an account that is not yours. You want the custodian to require your signature in order for funds to be moved out of your account.

For instance, I use two custodians, and there are times that I need a client to move money from the account at one custodian to their account at the other custodian. I can't do that for them. They can either login to the custodian website and initiate the transfer or they have to sign a form and transfer it.

2) Do not give anyone your log-in information

That raises another point: don't let the advisor or money manager have access to the log-in information you use to access the custodian website. First, they shouldn't need it because they should already have access to the same information. Second, most custodian websites give you the ability to initiate money or account transfers electronically. If you give the manager access to your password, you are giving them the ability to transfer your money anywhere they want!

A private money manager *will* require trading discretion in the account. That allows the manager to place trades, i.e., to buy and sell securities in your account without having to contact you before each trade. That is normal when working with a money manager, because that's what you are paying them to do. It's NOT normal when working with a traditional advisor, especially if the traditional advisor gets paid on commission.

You can limit the discretionary authority the money manager has by only allowing him or her to trade certain types of securities. For instance, if the money manager doesn't use futures, Forex or options, then s/he doesn't need discretion granted for them.

3) Beware of returns that are too good to be true.

It is extremely rare for ANY manager to provide market-bettering returns every year.

Bernie Madoff had 10+% returns year in and year out, yet rather than questioning how that could be possible, his clients just gave him more money!

Unless you are primarily invested in fixed-income products that pay a set rate of interest, you should expect variability of returns: they shouldn't be the same each quarter or each year. Interest rates and stock markets go up and down due to their cycles. Even if you are invested in individual bonds that pay a fixed rate of interest, the market value of those bonds is going to fluctuate. If you aren't seeing that fluctuation in your statements, ask questions.

4) Finally, you should be concerned if there AREN'T periods in which the value of your account goes down.

If the manager is investing in stocks, bonds or real estate, there will be times that losses will occur. The manager, hopefully, will be taking steps to try to minimize those losses, but no one is always right.

Conclusion

There are a lot of similarities between investing and losing weight. The secret to losing weight isn't finding some magic pill or crash diet; it's finding something that you can live with longterm. What works for someone else may not work for you. There are a lot of different diets to choose from, even a Twinkie diet! You have to ask yourself if that's something that you want to do longterm. For instance, there is a celery diet where all you eat is celery, but do you really want to live the rest of your life eating just celery?

It's the same way when it comes to investing. Just because something worked well for someone else doesn't mean it will work well for you. Your situation is different. Fluctuation in value that's tolerable for someone else may cause you to lose sleep.

In short, you have to find the approach to investing that's right for you. Some ways of investing are hard for people to stomach. If you use the wrong approach you won't be able to sustain it for the long term, so you won't get the results you need.

The key is to find something that works for you and your lifestyle, but above all make sure that you maintain control over your financial future and have the flexibility to easily change paths.

I'm someone whom my clients trust and turn to for help with any financial decision they make, but I am primarily a money manager. I realize that most components of someone's financial plan don't require a lot of ongoing work—except the management of their investments, and how well those investments are managed is the linchpin of their entire financial plan. If it's not done well, there's little point to the rest of the plan.

Unfortunately, I don't think the financial services industry does a good job for the individual investor. You don't have millions and millions of dollars, so your money isn't going to get personal attention-- except with someone who is a private money manager as I've described.

You aren't rich. Even having a million dollars nowadays doesn't make you rich, yet your money management needs are just as great, if not greater, than the super-rich because you have so few viable options.

There are thousands of people out there ready to take your money, earn a big commission off of you and move on, but that's not what you need. I think the more you get to know about a private money manager and what we do, the more you will realize that we offer something you can't find anywhere else. Is what we do for everybody? No. But it may be just what YOU are looking for.

Thank you for taking the time to read this book. I hope that it has been helpful. You can contact me at jeff@commonsenseadvisors.com.

A WORD ON FAITH

My faith is not something that I talk about regularly as a part of my position as a private money manager I've come across many advisors that wear their Christianity on their sleeve and seem to use it as part of their marketing, but I am often hesitant to even mention it unless the person I'm talking to brings it up. I guess I would rather my actions attest to my faith and values as opposed to my words.

I want to share briefly about my faith to give you a better understanding of whom I am and what motivates me. Since my faith undergirds everything I do, this is the one place that I'll talk about it in more depth.

I am a believer…a Christian. It wasn't always that way. I grew up knowing about God as a Catholic, but never really had a relationship with him. (I know plenty of Catholics that do have that relationship with God; I just didn't happen to be one of them at the time!) Looking back, though, I can see where He was working in my heart long before I asked him into my life during college.

Even as early as seventh grade I realized that I didn't have any true hope or purpose. I remember waking up in the morning thinking that life didn't really matter. I used to think, *You wake up, go to school, do homework, go to bed and repeat. Eventually you go to work instead of school, but it is still the same monotony.* OK, I probably didn't use the word "monotony"! I couldn't see the point, the purpose of life.

Early in my childhood, things were great. My dad was a corporate executive, we had a nice house and everything seemed easy. Then during the 1970s, all that changed. We moved 2-3 times to different parts of the country, but the recession continued to take its toll on our lifestyle. Like many in that decade, as a family we went from being upper-middle class to lower-middle class.

I was in fifth grade by that time, and the difficulties in my family were becoming more obvious to me. My two older brothers got into drugs and it became clear that one of them (my oldest brother) had a mental illness and was in and out of mental hospitals. That stressor, combined with the financial pressures related to the ongoing economic difficulties of the late 1970s, culminated in my parents getting a divorce.

By the time I was in high school, I was struggling to keep up appearances at school while trying to cope with what was going on at home. I was filled with fear and remember having a knot in my stomach every time my oldest brother was around. Socially I was awkward, and over time I was tormented by nightmares, which went on for years.

I was a confused young man with misplaced priorities. I was self-centered, egotistical on the outside but insecure and afraid on the inside. Thankfully, I never turned to drugs or alcohol—probably because I saw the results of that at home.

Into The "World"

I ended up going to a Christian college (Milligan College in TN) because I wanted to go where my best friend was going. It's funny, but I remember thinking that I could act like a Christian and fake my way through it! How funny.

Milligan College was like a different world to me and there weren't too many kids there like me. It became obvious how sheltered most of them were when, during the first week of my first semester, I let slip a very mild cuss word, only to witness the utter shock and horror of those at the table.

I was required to take a Bible class that first semester and it was the first time I began reading the Bible. The more I read, the more something was changing inside me. It was like the words were coming alive and touching something deep inside me—and that was reading Genesis!

The Holy Spirit continued to be at work in those first weeks of class and, in my heart, I found myself asking if He was real and then asking Him to show me that He was real. Within days of asking that question, my best friend and I went to a lookout at the second-highest mountain east of the Mississippi.

Being macho and self-centered, I decided we should do some rock climbing even though we didn't have any equipment with us. At one point I basically forced my friend to go from one ledge to a higher ledge when he didn't want to. I was already on the upper ledge, so I put my arm toward the lower ledge and told my friend to take my hand and I'd help him make it up. He did, but he didn't.

He did take my hand and I started pulling him up. He didn't make it to the upper ledge. He was just about there and let go of my hand to get a different handhold. That's when he lost his footing, dropped back to the small lower ledge and fell backward off the cliff. There I was, sitting with my hand still reaching out, watching him plunge to what would surely be his death.

He fell about 25-30 feet and landed on some rocks that had some leaves on them, only to tumble off of another ledge and fall another 30-40 feet. Eventually, he landed on some large boulders that had a thin layer of pine needles on them. When he landed on them, the whole bed of pine needles started sliding off those boulders, and the next landing would have been a couple hundred feet further down.

Suddenly, though, the sliding pine needles stopped and so did he. He was still moving, still looking up at me. I yelled at the top of my voice for him to stay there and I would be right down.

It's at that point that I knew, even though he was still alive, that I had lost his friendship forever. I was closer to him than I was to anyone else. He helped me survive through my troubled high school years. He was the one person I could depend on. He was the one person that understood me.

He was the reason I went to Milligan. And then, as I was trying to make my way down those cliffs, I just knew that the friendship was gone because it was my fault that he fell. It was my ego that pushed him to do something that he wasn't comfortable doing. I felt an incredible sense of shame and guilt.

Eventually I got down to him. To our amazement, after falling 75 feet and bouncing off a ledge along the way, and after landing on only a thin layer of pine needles on top of boulders, he had sustained only minor injuries (a few scrapes on his elbows)—unbelievable!

I led him back up to the lookout where we were at before my wonderful "Hey, let's go rock climbing" idea.

All the way back up to that platform, I just knew that he must have been furious with me because of what I had done. We were both silent most of the way up. Eventually, we got back to the platform and I realized that I had inadvertently left my camera down on the ledge from which he had fallen. I was going to go back down and get it, but he didn't want me to. Of course I insisted. He suggested that we pray first.

And it was his prayer that changed my life.

He started by thanking God that I was there; that I was there to help him get back to the top. I couldn't believe it. He wasn't mad at me—it hadn't even crossed his mind. Him thanking God for me? Didn't he realize it was my fault?

That night on the way down the mountain, I totaled my car in a freak accident. At that point I literally got out of the car, sat down in the middle of the country road we were on and said, "OK God, you've got my attention."

Well, there's much more to the story and I'll be happy to share it with you personally if you <u>ask</u>, but the next morning I was so broken emotionally that I couldn't go to class. I ended up in the chapel and basically said, "God, I've made a mess of my life the last 17 years, I know it's not worth much, but if you want it you can have it."

That's all it took. Within minutes all the fear that I had lived with for years was….gone. And it was replaced by a peace that I can't even begin to describe. It was the first time in my life that I felt free.

Most people stop there, but that's not the end of my story. Just because He was in my heart didn't mean that I lived happily ever after, but I did meet and marry the most incredible woman in the world. We decided we wanted the adventure track with God, and we've had many adventures together.

Still, I had a crisis of faith in the '90s that has taken me a while to recover from. My wife and I (and our first child) had returned from Hungary after serving as missionaries there for six months. We ended up starting a children's ministry where we wrote, directed and produced dramatized Bible stories on cassette tapes (yes, cassette tapes).

There I was doing what I felt was a ministry to children--while ignoring my own children. I was putting the ministry before my family and before my relationship with my wife. It was seven of the most difficult years of my life.

Through that crisis, though, He changed me. I was still very strong-willed, and it took that crisis and incredible pressure, me coming to the end of my rope, to finally cause me to let go and allow Him to change me.

In the same way that I am so thankful for my friend in college, I'm even more grateful to my wife for sticking with me during that time, and I'm especially grateful for the relationships I have with my children.

Since then our family has grown, to include a sibling group of three from Ethiopia. We've had the privilege of watching that same loving God heal and restore their hearts and minds and transform them into happy and healed children with a bright future and expectant hope.

We continue to be involved in missions, having been to Cambodia twice and establishing a long-term relationship with some special believers there. God has also knit us into a thriving community of believers in our area, where we are blessed to both give and receive.

Like I said at the beginning, my faith isn't something that I wear on my sleeve. It's the foundation of my life, my purpose, my reason for living.

My favorite verse of scripture is from John 6:36. It says, "The Spirit gives life; the flesh counts for nothing." My goal is to follow the Spirit of God completely, so His life can flow through mine.

Faith, Family, Finance. I'm a more effective private money manager because of that order. And a better father, husband and friend.

God Bless,

Jeff

www.ingramcontent.com/pod-product-compliance
Lightning Source LLC
Chambersburg PA
CBHW051736170526
45167CB00002B/952